Willie Park, jnr. in action; the world's first golf-course architect, who laid out the original course at Barnton Gate, for Bruntsfield, in 1898. With him is his renowned caddie Johnnie ('Fiery') Carey, also of Musselburgh Links, whose nickname derives from his complexion, not his manner. He featured in cigarette-cards of golfing notables, and is commemorated at Monktonhall golf course by the 'Fiery' 16th.
(Photo: Rev. Donald Lindgren).

BRUNTSFIELD LINKS
GOLFING SOCIETY
A SHORT HISTORY

BRUNTSFIELD LINKS GOLFING SOCIETY

A SHORT HISTORY

STEWART CRUDEN

THE BRUNTSFIELD LINKS GOLFING SOCIETY LIMITED
IN ASSOCIATION WITH
JOHN DONALD PUBLISHERS LIMITED
EDINBURGH

I've just one prayer, Ne'er change your name,
'Twill show what once has been;
A record that the King of games
Was played on Bruntsfield Green.

from 'Auld Bruntsfield's Lament'
by G. Lorimer
on the last page of
*Reminiscences of the Old Bruntsfield Links Golf Club
1866–1874*
by
Thomas S. Aitchison and George Lorimer
1902

© Stewart Cruden 1992

ISBN 0 85976 358 7

A catalogue record for this book
is available from the British Library.

Typeset by The Midlands Book Typesetting Company, Loughborough.
Printed in Great Britain by Courier International Ltd, East Kilbride.

Introduction

The Members of The Bruntsfield Links Golfing Society have every reason to be grateful to their predecessors for this inheritance, and fortunate that we have in Stewart Cruden an experienced historian to narrate the Society's history for us. He tells the story of the Society's beginnings at Bruntsfield Links, through its move to Musselburgh and its eventual arrival at Davidson's Mains. At times the records for the completion of the history have been meagre, but our historian has been painstaking in his research, and with great care, and many hours, he has produced an engaging work, which will be of great interest to those wishing to learn about the Society's part in the development of golf in Edinburgh, and to all lovers of The Bruntsfield Links Golfing Society.

The decisions taken as regards the various moves of the Society were not always unanimous, but when circumstances dictated the need for change, the Members of the day did not flinch from making those decisions; and we, the present Members, are the beneficiaries of their foresight, in that we now find ourselves in what must be one of the most attractive settings for a golf course in any city.

When looking out from the Clubhouse, over the Firth of Forth, one cannot help but be reminded of the story told by a former Captain, the late Alec Bateman, of the Texan visitor who enquired 'whether the pond was part of the course?'

Stewart Cruden answers the above question, and many others regarding the Society's history, but still leaves some for speculation, such as the date of the founding of the Society, which he surmises is a few years earlier than the heretofore accepted date.

The Society is a sociable body, where Members enjoy their golf, and from this history it appears that it was ever so. We are grateful to our predecessors for their careful management of the Society and to Stewart Cruden for this interesting and carefully researched history.

Ewen K. Cameron

Captain, 1989-91
The Bruntsfield Links Golfing Society

Preface

Voicing a proper concern at a deplorable historical omission I ventured to say that a Golfing Society which boasted '1761', and is arguably earlier, and is to be thought the fourth oldest in the world, ought to have a written History, whereupon certain members sufficiently persuaded but insufficiently reticent said, 'Good idea, why don't you do it?' This alarming response has generated much work and no little vexation of spirit, for the task has turned out to be not as simple as expected.

It happened at this time of fruitful thinking that the then Secretary, Mr M. W. Walton, drew my attention to three or four black, tin, deed boxes of a lawman's kind, which lay ignored but pregnant with possibilities, in the basement of the clubhouse. There they lay, neglected and unopenable until the exertions of a locksmith revealed their historical significance. It quite fortified my idea of how this History should, and could, be written, as continuity and narrative, not a passive record of events.

I had thought when toying with the subject and making desultory notes that, by reference to minute books, supplementary references to Clark's *Golf*, and by extensive reading of other printed books, that a reasonable History could be constructed. But the black deed boxes yielded original and authentic source material, not otherwise available, in the form of miscellaneous papers dating from 1808, all illustrative, in one way and another, of the Society's life at Bruntsfield Links in the nineteenth century. Nothing sensational is there to be found about a small Society meeting once a week, except perhaps six galls. best old whisky, £4.5.0, at the beginning of one month, ditto at the end of the next, and six bots. Bollinger £1.14.0, in between, and other startling facts of similar kind indicative of the Society's lifestyle, at least in certain respects. Enriching the collection in other ways are signatures of Old Tom Morris, McEwan, and Gourlay.

So the emphasis changed for the early period, about which nothing was known except that life began at Bruntsfield. The wealth of detailed information in these papers has amplified in full measure the account of Aitchison and Lorimer in their affectionate *Reminiscences*, and prompted inquiry into the whereabouts of that life, in the Register of Sasines in the Scottish Record Office, and in the Search Room of the City Archivist. The result of hopeful endeavour therein is the identification beyond reasonable doubt of the Society's first home, or perhaps its home at first remove from accommodation shared with neighbouring Burgess, a not unlikely possibility.

From Aitchison and Lorimer's *Reminiscences* and the Society's *ipsissima verba* of the minute books I have been much struck by a continuity of generous thoughts and considerations of good fellowship in membership and staff, who seem truly to be part of it, both 'in the Clubhouse and on the Green', as the Navy happily expressed it when acknowledging wartime hospitality. A recent recollection of a senior member tells all. It was, he said to me, thought to be a good idea to get a front carriage in the train to Davidson's Mains, for it was considered bad form to hurry past a fellow member on the way up to the clubhouse: about Bruntsfield's historic and continuing informality and friendliness no more need be said after that.

After much cogitation I have decided that neither reader nor publisher need be burdened with the effort and cost of a proliferation of footnotes and references proper to an academic History, which this is not, although it leans heavily upon writings of gravity and note. I owe much to *Golf in the Making*, by Ian T. Henderson and David I. Stirk (1979), a remarkable and truly original book, constantly within arm's length for its hard facts, illustrations, and historical observations; and I have plundered *Golf, a Royal and Ancient Game*, by R. Clark (1875), a historical account of Scottish golf with invaluable 'Extracts' from the minute or record books of the Honourable Company, the R & A, the Royal Musselburgh and the Bruntsfield Links and Burgess Societies. This book is particularly valuable for Bruntsfield, whose surviving minute books begin at the end of 1874, for Clark's 'Extracts' redeem the woeful history of the Society's records and carry it back to 1787, compensating for those lost.

Further evidence if not proof of early Bruntsfield minute books is discussed in the early pages of the *Reminiscences* and by a divine dispensation of Providence a small paper in the collection excavated from the aforesaid black, tin, deed boxes, is an account dated March 1864, from a George Street firm of Edinburgh stationers, for embossing titles on the spine of 'Minute Book vol. 5'. That means there were five good volumes of Minutes by 1864, for many years before the surviving series begins.

I have also read with much profit *Edinburgh, the Story of a City*, by E. F. Catford (1975), and *The Making of Classical Edinburgh*, by Professor A. J. Youngson (1966). *Famous Scottish Links* by T. D. Miller (1911), and *Edinburgh in the Nineteenth Century*, ed. W. M. Gilbert (1901), have also yielded information, as has the majesterial *Golf Book of East Lothian*, by the Rev. John Kerr (1896). The picture of the Golf Hotel, or Tavern, (Plate 4), is taken from the Burgess *Chronicle*, for which acknowledgement is gratefully rendered. Three recent publications insist on recognition: *The Parks of Musselburgh; Golfers, Architects, Clubmakers*, by John Adams (1991). *Colt & Co; Golf Course Architects*, by Fred Hawtree (1991). *Golf on Gullane Hill*, by Archie Baird (1982, 1989).

The Edinburgh City Archivist, Mr Arnott Wilson, and his assistant, Mrs Margaret McBride, gave me much help and themselves much trouble in producing remote and dusty volumes of Valuation Rolls, Dean of Guild Petitions with architect's drawings, and the like. Without their genial courtesy the early domestic history of the Society at Wright's Houses, Bruntsfield Links, arguably the most important part of the book, could never have been written. I am indebted also for the advice of Lt Cdr D. Currie, RN (Retd), and to the helpful interest of the Rev. Donald Lindgren, of the Congregational Church in Musselburgh, for the use of illustrations from his two books *Musselburgh in Old Picture Postcards* (1987 and 1989), published by European Library – Zaltbommel/Netherlands.

Mr. Colledge of Mortonhall, presently engaged in a history of that Club, which is heading for its centenary, has kindly written to inform me that Mr W. B. Taylor, architect of the Bruntsfield Clubhouse and conspicuously a Bruntsfield man, was no less conspicuously a Mortonhall man also.

Photographs, original, as for the cover, and for reproduction, are by Mr Bill Stout, Photographer PR Press, Edinburgh. Grateful acknowledgement of his contribution is extended to the publishers for their cooperation in all respects.

I must record my appreciation of Council's approval of this endeavour. I am grateful to Mr M. W. Walton who was the Society's Secretary while the book was being constructed, for his practical interest and encouragement then, and since, in the hurly-burly of publication. I am more than grateful to him for allowing a wayward author unrestricted access to his personal secretary for typing help, a freedom which his successor, Lt Col Hext, has unhesitatingly continued. Thus has Margaret Johnston typed and retyped every word. Without her help, in the various stages of writing and rewriting, shortening and expanding, recasting and writing all over again, this book, which the author hopes will be judged with forbearance and charity, would never have been finished at all.

Edinburgh, 1991   *Stewart Cruden*

Contents

CHAPTER 1

Life at Bruntsfield Links

Almost in the heart of Edinburgh, in these days of its extension, is Bruntsfield Links, once the scene of much fine golf, but where few matches are now played, and those few much to the peril of the populace.

So wrote Horace Hutchinson, Amateur Champion in 1886, the first English-man to captain the R & A, in his classic *Golf*, published in 1890 in the 'Badminton Library of Sports and Pastimes'.

Golf is still played there, after a fashion and rarely to the peril of the populace, by the diminishing membership of the Veterans' Short Hole Club, whose clubhouse is a small wooden hut on the north side of the links, at the western end. The interior of the clubhouse is no more indulgent than the exterior suggests it might be, a table and a chair or two, and some golfing mementoes, serve the members very well. This unpretentious clubhouse, and the members who use it, exemplify the very spirit of the game, and perpetuate the continuity of golf on Bruntsfield Links in an authentic history of more than three hundred years, and a probable history stretching as far back as the middle of the fifteenth century, when an Act of Parliament in 1457 (James II) was severe in discouragement of golf and football and decreed and ordained that 'the futeball and the golfe be utterly cryit doune' in favour of national defence and needful practice of archery, then being neglected, for opposing 'our auld enemies of England'.

The daily play of the Veterans, weather permitting, allows the contempla-tive wanderer over the links today at least to imagine groups of golfers hard at work, who eventually, drawn together by the inclinations of companionship, formed themselves into golfing societies and clubs.

Early drawings and paintings give remarkable and convincing pictures of Bruntsfield Links in the eighteenth century (Plates 2 and 3). There are no whin bushes today, nor trees, and the mounds and hollows are neither so high nor so deep as Ewbank and Slack show them, and there are few indications of the small quarry pits which in 1695 the Town Council permitted the Tacksman of Bruntsfield Links to dig on condition that his permissible acre of development was 'ane distance from the place where the neighbours play at Goulf'—but six years later he was found to have excavated quarries

1

which 'spoyled the Gouffing' and endangered those others who passed by. Evidently golf at Bruntsfield Links was an eventful and uncertain activity in the eighteenth century. It always is, of course.

The conditions of a Public Roup at Bruntsfield Links, or the Burgh Muir, in November 1738, give us some idea of what manner of men they were who founded the Society with the intentions of today, but in circumstances very different:

> The Magistrates and Council reserve to themselves and their successors and the whole inhabitants of the City of Edinburgh and Libertys thereof full powers to use the exercise of Golf and Walking upon the said Links any time of the year, also clothes drying [*When a ball is on clothes or within a club-length of a washing-tub the clothes may be drawn from under the ball and the tub may be removed*, opined the R & A in 1851], the use of natural spring water, the making of holes and burying the dead in case of plague, and the mustering of the city Train bands, Guards, Militia and fencible men of His Majesty's regular Forces.

The plague, 'Asiatic Cholera', made its appearance in Edinburgh in January 1832. February 9 was observed as a local day of prayer; thousands died of it in Edinburgh that year. Leith Links, where golf was played, duels fought, deserters shot, and plague victims buried, was similarly affected.

So, in their abbreviated game the Veterans continue an essential part of Edinburgh's social history. Not that the passers-by, the vociferous and agitated schoolchildren, the young mums pushing prams and citizens just out for a walk would know that, or even know that they were playing golf for that matter, but the Veterans deserve an honourable mention, for Bruntsfield Links is one of the oldest links in the world where golf is still played. Scarcely is a city so handsomely provided. One ventures to say that there are more first-class courses within the Edinburgh city boundaries than there are within the boundaries of any other city in the world.

The early Bruntsfield Links Golfing Society, and others, used the Links 'for the healthful exercise of Golf', notably the Burgess, the Allied, the St Leonards and the Merchiston clubs. Burgess and Bruntsfield eventually moved away from the links of Bruntsfield to those of Musselburgh, where each built a clubhouse of no ordinary merit, then separately they returned to Edinburgh and fortuitously resumed a long and neighbourly relationship 'in cordiality and good understanding' which subsists to this day. Rarely if ever have the histories of two ancient clubs been so distinct and so close.

The Allied was founded in 1856 by a few who had served on the Allied side (hence the name) in the recent Crimean War. It survives, actively, to this day, one of the oldest non-course-owning clubs in existence. We are informed by its secretary that the early minutes are in the City Library, and that one records a resolution to pay for street lamps broken in the playing of golf, and another the abandonment of the stymie, because it engendered bad feeling, many years before the R & A was similarly enlightened in 1951. But only the Bruntsfield Links Golfing Society has kept the name alive since earliest times, without recourse to resurrection.

It is a name worth keeping. All honour to the memory of the men who kept it and ensured its place in the early history of golf. We like to think that there should be significance in the retention of the name, that it is the senior club which retains it and the splinter groups which lose it. Nothing is more plausible than this hypothesis, but there is no evidence to support such a tempting assumption, for the two contestants for seniority are the Bruntsfield Links Society and the Burgess Society and both were so named long before they formally quit the Links of Bruntsfield for those of Musselburgh in the later nineteenth century when, after a hundred years and more, play on their home green became difficult, congested, and perhaps much to the peril of the populace.

Wright's Houses and the Original Clubhouse

The social and golfing address of the various Bruntsfield golfers was some-where in Wright's Houses. The 'Index of Edinburgh Places, 1781–1820', housed in the Scottish Record Office, has an enormous 'Wright's Houses' entry. A brief mention of that locality might here be given, for the golfers played a significant part in the development of Wright's Houses, referred to in the Register of Sasines 1791 as 'near Edinburgh'.

In the eighteenth century, and indeed before that, 'The High Way', the main road to Edinburgh from Fairmilehead, West Linton and the south, passed through a small country village known as Wright's Houses at the west end of the wilderness of the Burgh Muir. The village took its name from Wryt's House, a country mansion which overlooked Bruntsfield Links. The village which grew round the big house was largely demolished in 1794 when the road was widened. The house was demolished in 1800, being 'hideous' (which it was not), and was soon succeeded on the same site by the Hospital of James Gillespie of Spylaw, who ground snuff and made a fortune and had a carriage. 'Wha wad hae thocht it that noses had bocht it' wrote Henry Erskine unkindly.

That part of the village on the west side of the road which is now Bruntsfield Place has almost entirely been replaced in later urban extension of the city. Only a little lane and a few rather good small houses at the top of

Hailes Street remain. The old Toll Bar of today stands opposite the original Toll Bar of Wright's Houses. Apart from those few remains of the village only the Golf Tavern survives, and it has been much altered and renamed.

The village spread eastwards across the road which is now Bruntsfield Place and that part of it which served the golfers and still overlooks the Links is the long narrow built-up 'island' which is distinguished by the powerful Barclay Church (1862) at one end, two splendid tenement blocks, and the Golf Tavern.

It was in this eastern half of the village, overlooking the Links, that the various golfing societies, such as they were in the eighteenth century, had their rendezvous, which varied as they did. It is indeed a remarkable fact of Scottish social and sporting history which authenticates the playing of golf as early as the fifteenth century, that until the 1880s, when there was a veritable explosion of golf, few, if any, golfing societies owned the greens they played over. Nor did they have clubhouses. They availed themselves of taverns or houses conveniently near. The Honourable Company of Edinburgh Golfers at Leith Links (never Bruntsfield Links), the Burgess and the Bruntsfield Societies, were eventually pioneers in the building of private clubhouses, and that comparatively late in their history.

It was the custom of early golfers, before they consciously organised themselves into Societies or Clubs, to foregather regularly in a tavern and, if they were sufficiently established, to reserve therein a private room continually, or to take a room or rooms in a tenement with a neighbourly housekeeper. The latter arrangement was certainly the case with the Bruntsfield Links Society for a hundred Bruntsfield years or more, as the *Reminiscences* testify. That book includes a lively and circumstantial account of the Society's life at that time, and in light-hearted veracity races along as follows:

> In those days, the club met in a house facing the Links, close to the old Golf Tavern, which formed the headquarters of the Burgess Golf Club. It consisted of ground floor and sunk flat, the latter being occupied by Mrs Stewart, who took charge of the premises, and attended to our comforts on the occasion of our dinners. For our own use we had one long, low-roofed room. Originally there were two, with an intervening passage, but the partitions had been cleared away. That one room was all we had. In one corner was an arrangement of basins behind a screen, which served the purpose of a lavatory; in another stood a cupboard, in which, along with a plentiful supply of plates and glasses, were to be found the various kinds of liquid refreshment most in demand, together with bread and cheese and biscuits, in addition to which there was usually a cask of draught ale on tap, which stood beside one of the windows. To these good things we helped ourselves, dropping the equivalent into a box which stood on the mantelpiece; but it was a most unsatisfactory mode of procedure, for the box could not give change, and so payment had often to be postponed to the occasion of the next visit, when

it was perhaps forgotten. There was an ever-recurring deficit in regard to which every treasurer in turn made his protest.

This account covers a period of ten years (1866–74), and is of fairly late date in the Society's existence. But ten years in the mid-nineteenth century were longer than a decade in the hastening world of the twentieth, and the situation here described could well be applied to earlier and later Bruntsfield life and circumstances.

Otherwise, taverns were resorted to. They were generally known by the name of the proprietor. Hence 'Luckie Clephan's', 'Barry's', 'Mrs Forman's', 'Thomas Comb's', 'McKendrick's', 'Steven's', and others too numerous to mention, in Edinburgh, Leith, and Musselburgh.

John Clephan was a clubmaker, registered as such in Leith Records 1725–50, and a golfer of some local renown. His tavern was in the Kirkgate, now demolished. Thereto the Honourable Company resorted, with a locker-room and a dining-room of their own, until in 1768 they built a Golf House. It was in the south-west corner of the Links, where the course, or green, of Leith Links is commemorated at Duncan Place, which runs through the Links, by a small stone cairn. It bears two metal plates engraved with a brief history of the Links and that famous club, and a line drawing of the course they played on there, five holes of four hundred yards, where there were to be seen 'the greatest and the wisest in the land mingling freely with the humblest mechanics'.

But far on the other side of the city the Bruntsfield golfers found shelter in sundry 'howffs', of which, as Mr Cameron Robbie points out in his Burgess *Chronicle*, that of Maggie Johnstone, who died in 1711, was most renowned, and commemorated in moving terms by Allan Ramsay, thus:

When we were wearied of the gowff,
Then Maggie Johnstone's was our howff.

The sentiments here expressed in verse suggest perhaps a more decorous and homely *après-golf* than does the East Lothian Golf Club's Minute which requires the landlord of the Golf Hotel, Gullane, to provide not only Sheep's Head and Haggis at the next meeting but to have his whisky and sherry in decanters not so like each other, as after a certain period in the evening some of the members found it difficult to distinguish which was which. The picture thus suggested goes far to support a suspicion of golfing propensities first suspected by the present writer after coming across a Minute of the Musselburgh Club which records with creditable candour a brief but telling account of a meeting in 1793 which 'was so merry that it was agreed that matching and every other business should be delayed till next month'.

But if howffs and taverns were indispensable features in the golfing scene and the Bruntsfield Links Society of small parade strength mustering once a week, could order 6 galls. best whisky at the beginning of one month and ditto at the end of the next, plus a 1/2 doz. Bollinger in between, we may well believe Bruntsfield's regrettable admission that 'we did not come for golf alone'.

In a wide variety of miscellaneous papers, some seventeen hundred in twenty-three bundles, which four black tin deed boxes have preserved for us and recently yielded up their contents, there are tradesmens' bills for curtains, carpets, wallpaper, chairs and tables, door locks and door bells, etc., and the name of Mrs Stewart is of frequent occurrence from 1863 until 15 December 1882 when the Bruntsfield Clubhouse changed hands and there was much argument in high places about finally quitting Bruntsfield altogether and settling in Musselburgh. Mrs Stewart was evidently an active and efficient housekeeper, as one of the Society's earliest existing minutes amply testifies:

> The wines, beer and spirits were to be in the charge of Mrs Stewart, housekeeper, who was authorised to serve out from time to time in small quantities as required and along with the Treasurer to keep a constant watch upon the Box, and the Council hopes that members will be diligent in paying for refreshments, otherwise it would be necessary to establish a Bar, which would be expensive and inconvenient and besides would materially interfere with the amenity of the place.

Evidently Mrs Stewart, like Mr Guppy's mother in *Bleak House*, was 'one who could be freely trusted with wines, spirits and malt liquors'. She was rewarded by a gift for her long service, which must have begun before 1863, the date of the earliest surviving papers addressed specifically to her. They come from fishmongers, from butchers, bakers and tradesmen, for papering and panelling a fire screen, for repairing a door bell, laying linoleum. Her salary was £15 p.a., paid in two instalments of £7.10/-.

The historically-minded or economical reader seeking easy justification for hoarding, for throwing nothing away, however trivial, need look no further than those four black, tin, deed boxes. The miscellaneous papers therein have yielded valuable information and proof, not otherwise obtainable, of the Society's domestic life at Bruntsfield and Musselburgh.

But as well, they have yielded up the oldest authentic records of the Society. They are not discursive as *Reminiscences* is, but they ante-date that cheerful and informative book by fifty years. They consist of a few casual handwritten papers, 'memos' such as a secretary or clubmaster would write, and they are dated, even those that are scribbled, a most excellent thing. By great good fortune these few have survived. They begin with a small scrap of paper headed 'Deficients for 1808 & 1809—Mr Reid two years 1.15.0., Mr Trotter 3 years 2.12.6, Mr Frank Anderson do 2.12.6, Mr Campbell Gardner, entry money 1.1.6., contribution 0.8.0, Box Money 0.2.0.' But on the other side of this scrap of paper, headed 'Deficients for 1808, 1809, 1810 & 1811', we see that Messrs. Reid, Trotter, and Anderson had 'given up', having added a year to their debts. In 1811 two named 'contributions' are 17/6 each, and there are incidental notes and receipts, of which two from Daniel Lizars are curiously interesting, being for the printing of '300 golfing letters', (17/6 in 1810), and the printing of '500 golfing letters', (£1.2.3 in 1812). This seems excessive as regards numbers, but such are the facts. Payments of Box Money, at 2/6 for 1811 and 1812, are receipted by Mrs Henderson, seemingly a housekeeper, an early Mrs Stewart. In 1812 she received an honorarium of three guineas. In 1801 she featured in a matter of some esoteric interest today, worthy of remark.

According to a Bruntsfield minute of October 1801, which is reproduced in Clark's *Golf*, she was authorised 'to buy a dozen caps and aprons'. This brief observation, repeated at large without critical detachment, has recently stimulated assertions about the rôle of Masons in early Scottish golfing history. As it concerns Bruntsfield particularly, with an alleged indication of masonic custom, it has received our respectful consideration and research. Diligent and serious investigation has produced no evidence of masonic influences however. Far from it. It is moreover unlikely that a housekeeper would be charged by the Council of the Society with a task of masonic significance. It is more likely that her task was to purchase caps and aprons for herself and kitchen staff.

Among the above-mentioned scraps of paper are three sheets of more than passing interest. They are set out in similar style and by the same hand, in careful copperplate writing. The first is headed 'Bruntsfield Links Golfing Society, Contributions from 23 January 1812 to January 1813', and it is tabulated with Names against Debtor and Creditor columns: Box money is 2/6, 'contributions' (i.e. subscriptions presumably) is 15/- : there are eighteen names, properly listed with recorded payments. The second paper looks like a rough draft for a third, which is identical, for 1813–14, with the same seventeen Names; but, the subscription has gone up to 17/6.

We may confidently conclude that in the early years of the nineteenth century the Society at Bruntsfield was a good-going concern and had consolidated its origins of fifty or more years earlier, and was now sufficiently well established and organised to muster seventeen 'regulars'. The modest roll-call need occasion no surprise. Fifty years later the membership was still limited, now to fifty-five, according to a detailed nominal roll of 1866.

More primary evidence of early date is enclosed in a small and flimsy brown paper cover. It is a pamphlet, undated, and without notice of its printer, nor indeed anything of its origins. But it is well and properly printed, and nicely sewn into the paper cover. It is of high historical interest to Bruntsfield golfers, to whom it is addressed: we might well add, to whom it is emphatically addressed. It is in two parts. The first, tersely and with no wasted words, codifies the etiquette and rules of play 'to be observed by the Bruntsfield Links Golfing Society when playing the Game'. The second part enshrines conditions affecting play for the Gold Medal, the Society's earliest and most prestigious trophy for play at Bruntsfield Links. We see that it was to be played for twice a year, in full uniform, over two rounds, (cf.map of course, Plate 8).

There is much to ponder over in the reading of those two Regulations. They must refer to a period between 1819 when the Medal was instituted, and 1871 when play for it was transferred to Musselburgh, an occasion which grieved old Bruntsfield hands, who felt it was 'breaking with old traditions in a sad way', but the Regulations observe the earliest rules of golf, upon which all subsequent rules have been based, which were drawn up in 1744 by the Gentlemen Golfers, the Honourable Company. To those original Rules amendments have of course been made.

Mr George Pottinger, in his comprehensive discussion and analysis of the original rules of golf and their amendments, in his *Muirfield and the Honourable Company*, draws attention to variations of 1809 which were obviously related to conditions at Leith Links which was the home of the Honourable Company at the time, as Bruntsfield Links was of the Society. The phraseology of the variation of 1809 is identical in some significant respects to that of the Regulations for the Bruntsfield golfers, for example 'if a ball sticks fast to the ground it must be loosened'. Such coincidences cannot be accidental. The Regulations here included are probably the original rules for the Gold Medal of 1819.

RULES AND REGULATIONS
To be Observed
BY THE MEMBERS OF THE BRUNTSFIELD

LINKS

GOLFING SOCIETY,

When playing the Game; and, also, when playing for

THE GOLD MEDAL

1. No Golfer, or Cadie, to be allowed to dig tee within ten yards of the hole, and no ball to be teed nearer the hole than two club lengths, nor farther from it than four, and the ball to be teed on the ground.

2. Two or more parties meeting at the hole, the party who plays first to be allowed to play their second strokes before the succeeding party strikes off. But should the first party's ball be a hazard, they shall stand aside till the second party passes them.

3. Every hole must be played out with the same ball that is struck from the tee, and no obstructions of any kind to be removed, but the ball must be played wherever it lies, unless in the water tract, when the player may lift his ball, drop it over his shoulder behind the hazard, and play it with an iron.

4. No hole is gained unless the ball is not of the party, that ball must be played from where-ever it is so struck or moved to.

7. In a match of more than two players, if a ball is struck twice, or oftener, successively by one player, that side of the match loses the hole.

8. If a party plays the adversary's ball, the adversary gains the hole.

9. If a party personally, or by his Cadie, stops or touches any ball of the match, the adversary gains the hole.

10. If a ball sticks fast into the ground it must be loosened, and the opposite party may insist to do so.

11. In playing for prizes, no competition to be allowed unless the parties are dressed in the uniform of the Society.

12. In *putting*, the ball, if practicable, is to be played directly for the hole, but if the adversary's ball opposes the player it shall be lawful to play upon it.

13. That when a match is taken at a monthly or quarterly meeting of the Club, a day shall be fixed for its being played, and the party failing to appear shall lose it, unless an apology is sent to the opponent the day before the match is to be played.

REGULATIONS

To Be Observed When Playing for
the

GOLD MEDAL

1. That the Medal shall be played for twice a year, viz. on the last Saturday of March and last Saturday of September; and the Candidate holing in two rounds at the fewest number of strokes shall be the winner. The winner shall not be allowed to play for the Medal again until one year after he has gained it twice successively.

2. That no Member who is in arrears to the Society shall be allowed to play for the Medal.

3. That the competitors shall play in single parties, and each party shall have a marker along with it, and if it shall happen that any Member wishing to compete for the Medal is without a partner, such Member shall be allowed to play by himself, and to take a marker along with him.

4. That a player may at any time lift his ball upon losing a stroke, and dropping the ball over his shoulder being the hazard.

5. That if, in playing through the green, a ball shall go into the whins, the water, the park, or shall be lost, the striker may return to the place as nearly as possible from whence the ball was struck, when he shall drop it, if found, over his shoulder; but if lost, another ball, in the same manner, and lose a stroke.

6. That in playing through the green, all loose stones and sticks, filth, nuisance, or other moveable impediments, and the balls, if they should happen to lie so close as not be played, shall be removed.

7. That no Member shall be allowed to compete for the Medal unless dressed in the full uniform of the Society.

8. That the winner of the Medal shall be obliged to wear it, suspended by a ribbon, round his neck, at the Annual Meeting, and on each Saturday of the Meeting of the Society during the year, and, at his option, every Saturday in the green.

9. The ball be teed within four club-lengths of the hole.

10. The Member gaining the Medal shall sign a receipt in the minute-book, obliging him and his heirs to return it to the Society at the expiry of Six Months from the time he receives it.

An entry in the Register of Sasines in the Scottish Record Office is headed 'Feb 3 1761', and says with official brevity, 'In a tenement at Bruntsfield Links called Foxtoun, Thomas Comb clubmaker, Wrights Houses'. This is of particular interest because the earliest authenticated minute of the Bruntsfield Links Golfing Society is place-dated 'Bruntsfield Links 10th June 1787, in Thos Comb's.' Evidently the Society had an early rendezvous in his part of a tenement called Foxtoun, near Edinburgh. In 1773 the Burgess golfers were also in Thomas Comb's, 'clubmaker, Bruntsfield Links or Wright's Houses, near Edinburgh', for weekly meetings, which they seemingly continued thereat, whereas the Bruntsfield golfers are later, in a different building nearby. It seems that the two Societies either shared accommodation or had adjacent accommodation in Thomas Comb's premises until around 1788, when the Bruntsfield Links Minutes cease to mention the name and merely record date and place, 'Bruntsfield Links'.

The ensuing minutes in Clark's *Golf*, which we must perforce regard as 'secondary' information but readily accept as authentic, are rich in expressions of conviviality and much harmony as they record clubable dining-out, 'at the University Tavern' (1830), and 'at Goodsman's Rooms', Wright's Houses (1842), where they penned a typically convivial and appreciative minute, which it is worth repeating here for the enigmatic statement it makes. It goes as follows:

Bruntsfield Links, 17th Dec. 1842

Matches were then arranged (handicap) to compete for the Prize Clubs presented by Mr Stewart, and after a keen and spirited contest Captain Mitchell was found to be the gainer, having holed the two rounds in 57 strokes.

A large party afterwards dined at Goodsman's, and spent a very happy evening, not the less so that some Member, to the company unknown, made the handsome present of half-a-dozen of Champagne. Mr Brown, after some very apposite remarks, read an interesting paragraph from the Bombay Times of the 19th October last, noticing certain proceedings of a golf Club formed in the East Indies, which gave rise to much felicitous discussion, and the appointment of a deputation, consisting of the Captain and Mr Paterson, to meet and compete with the like, or any number, of the Indian Club,—the deputation to travel at the Club's expense and by the new Aerial Transit, which is expected to start early in February next.

In the course of the evening the Secretary, Mr Donaldson, intimated that he intended presenting the club with a Silver Quaih to be competed for annually by handicap.

The meeting, which had been kept up with great spirit, then separated.

J.D., Sec.

What does this mean? What was the new Aerial Transit due to start next February, 1843? It is uncannily prophetic. Did it mean anything in 'much felicitous discussion'? Is it a champagne-related joke which should not have been minuted at all?

Robert Goodsman was a tenant and a proprietor of property in Wright's Houses, 'in the middle of the row facing the Links'. In 1932, it was reported to be standing, 'late Georgian, occupied by Gilchrist's Tavern, 31 Wright's Houses'. In 1852, pursuant to a meeting of the Council, the Captain privately interviewed Mrs Gilchrist as to her intention 'in regard to the occupation of the house'. After a confidential discussion it was agreed that the club would pay £9.14.0 of annual rent and Mrs Gilchrist would pay the remaining £5.

There can be little doubt that in the formative years of the Society's existence this house, 'facing the links', contained several dwellings, including the Bruntsfield Clubhouse, Gilchrist's Tavern, and eventually the 'Golf Tavern' of today.

The miscellaneous papers referred to above are of domestic interest and cover the period recalled by Aitchison and Lorimer, roughly 1860–80. They are variously addressed to The Golf House, The Club House, The Auld Hoose, The Bruntsfield Links Golfing Society, Wright's Houses, and the like, all sufficiently exact and recognisable by the Post Office and near-dwellers in a semi-rural environment. More to the point, among the contents of the deed boxes is an abundance of assessments and formal demands for rates and taxes delivered with official regularity to 30 and/or 31 Wright's Houses, while a series of receipts from the Superior's Factor which date from 1863 for half-yearly rents, are for 'a house 31 Wrights Houses as possessed by them'. And that house, as possessed by them, is sometimes designated '30 Wrights Hoses' in the same Factor's receipts.

It is evident in the foregoing indications, however inconclusive each might separately be, that in the eighteenth century the Society flourished at Bruntsfield Links and along with the Burgess resorted to Thomas Comb's, and thereafter at an address mostly in 30 and/or 31 Wright's Houses, that it had a permanent resident clubmistress, Mrs Stewart, who served it well for twenty years or more, and that, as the *Reminiscences* describes, it made a convivial and clubbable existence in an amalgamation of two or more apartments contrived by the removal of partitions, which were in all probability lath-and-plaster walls separating one dwelling from another in the manner all too frequent in the overcrowded tenements of old Edinburgh. And thereby hangs a tale.

According to the valuation rolls of the period, the community of Wright's Houses in the first half of the nineteenth century included, tenements which in one way and another housed a wide variety of occupants, who were the golfers' neighbours, such as: a grocer, engraver, clerk of works, coachsmith, printer, porter, wright, saddler, coachman, butler, tavern keeper, map mounter, macer, draughtsman, tailor, and labourer. The situation at Wright's Houses then, albeit in rural Edinburgh, was little better than that which prevailed in the congested city itself, concerning which the Census of 1851 showed that in the past fifty years the population of the Old Town had increased by 50 per cent from 20,000 to 30,000, without increase of houses, so that division and sub-division of existing property were inevitable. In fact, a crudely sub-divided house could contain many dwelling and have different numbers accordingly. Catford, in his *Edinburgh*, recounts a story of a tenant in the Lawnmarket who was alleged to have removed a partition from the adjacent dwelling on the same floor during its proprietor's absence, to add a room to his own; 'Stealing a room', as Henry Mackenzie called this form of conveyancing in his *Anecdotes and Egotisms* of 1825.

The tenement 'Foxton' or 'Golfhall' is not identifiable. It seems entirely to have been demolished. As we have observed, the only substantial part of the historic village of Wright's Houses which remains is the 'Golf Tavern' of today and this building has inevitably been somewhat altered, especially in the ground-floor public-house, part of which was given a new Tudor look in red sandstone with fine fenestration and detailing, and a splendid doorway with a cartouche, over which appear the golfers' prayerful words 'Far and Sure'. This was done with a contemporary interior in 1899, by R.M. Cameron, the architect who had done the Burgess Clubhouse at Barnton in best harled and half-timbered Jacobean three years before. (He also did the 'Guildford Arms' in West Register St and the 'Northern' at the corner of Warriston Crescent, in recognisable style, and other good works, not all public houses).

In the records of the City Archivist there is a petition dated March/April 1899 to the Dean of Guild Court concerning alterations and reconstruction at the Golf Tavern, 'All such operations confined to the property [sic] Nos. 30 and 31 Wright's Houses'. There are accompanying plans, sections and elevations, from 24 George St Edinburgh, and a site plan showing 'New Golf Tavern Bruntsfield Links'. The ground floor was to be as it is today but on the façade facing the Links the first and second floors and dormers are shown in the drawings to be very fanciful with projecting bay windows surmounted by pedimented gables. Fortunately, we think, this was never done. Also, in a Petition of Feb/March 1902, the petitioner assures the Dean of Guild Court that 'he is tenant of the Golf House Tavern Nos.30 and 31 Wrights Houses, Edinburgh, and has the consent of the proprietor to the foregoing alterations', (merely to extend back 15 ft.). Against the north wall of the tavern there remains today the street doorway of the stair which served the first and second floor private rooms over the public bar below. (Plates 6, 7).

Conspicuous among the many fine trophies in the Society's collection is the Gilmour Cup for the winter Hole and Hole Tournament, presented to the Society by ex-Captain Gilmour in 1901. The large cup (it is in fact a large bowl) is embellished in relief with a representation of part of Wright's Houses, being a translation by a skilled silversmith of a conflation of two pictures which separately feature the gable-end of an hotel and the façade of an adjacent house, both overlooking the Links.

Early drawings and paintings show the gable of the hotel with two pairs of windows. Between the upper pair and the lower pair a painted or boarded sign crosses the gable from side to side. The sign bears the words 'Golf Hotel', and between the words two crossed clubs with three balls between them. There is a water-colour of this in the public bar of the 'Golf Tavern' of today, and in the Veterans' Clubhouse, and the picture is reproduced in the Burgess *Chronicle* at the beginning of the chapter 'Early meeting-places of the Burgess', where it is captioned 'Golf Tavern, Bruntsfield Links (Plate 4). This was the home of the Burgess golfers in their early days. It has long been demolished.

Close to this hotel, in the embellishment of the Gilmour Cup, is a house of early nineteenth-century aspect. This became the 'Golf Tavern' of today, formerly 30 and 31 Wright's Houses, where the Bruntsfield golfers met, 'in a house facing the Links, close to the old Tavern which formed the headquarters of the Burgess Golf Club' (plates 5 and 6).

The *Reminiscences* of Aitchison and Lorimer cover twenty years of membership and relate much that is ephemeral and anecdotal, but it is related with authority and accuracy and enriched with shrewd character sketches. The authors contribute invaluable information about the clubhouse at Bruntsfield, where it was, and the life therein, and about the Links, the field of play, and how the golfers went about it. No other description of play over those historic links has come down to us, and from this unique account, which is sufficiently detailed, a map (Plate 8), was prepared by E.J. MacRae, the City Architect, in 1944, for the Royal Burgess Society. It is respectfully dedicated to William Breck Torrance, Captain of that Society, 1938–44, by the Captains of the Burgess, Bruntsfield, Warrender, and Merchiston Clubs, whose signatures were added below the dedication. The basic map is one of 1864 to which the golfing lay-out has been superimposed according to the Aitchison/Lorimer account. Sundry pleasing sketches suitable to the occasion have also been added to enliven the gift, and one of them is of particular interest in the present discussion because it is captioned 'Golf House, Wright's Houses, Bruntsfield Links, 1792'. It is a careful drawing of the gable-end of the Golf Hotel and is likely to be a copy of the water-colour painting of it. Placed as it is, in such a presentation as this, it is presumptive evidence that the Golf Hotel of the picture was the home of the Burgess Society which started a long occupation in 1792, the year given in the caption.

The map, a part of which we here reproduce to show the original lay-out of this historic green, shows the 1st Tee a little way up the Loaning Road, and the 1st hole, *c.* 270 yards, at the furthest or eastmost end of the Links, then uphill and westwards to the 2nd by View Park School (latterly James Gillespie's, now Boroughmuir School Annexe), then, for the 3rd, across the road and up towards the far south corner of the links, by the Bruntsfield Hospital, then back towards the clubhouse for the 4th and short 5th, and finally to the 6th in front of Glengyle Terrace, where Douglas McEwan, clubmaker, had his shop.

Such was the green in the mid-nineteenth century. Previously, until 1818, it consisted of five holes only, but in that year a sixth was won 'at the south end of the Links' by the hospital. The new ground was opened for play on 4 June 1818 and on that day there was a contest, Captain Gardner and Mr Graham of Bruntsfield versus Captain Duncan and Mr Edington of Burgess. The match was won by the Bruntsfield golfers whose Captain proposed that in future the new hole should be called the 'Union' hole, so named to commemorate the occasion and a mutual desire to consolidate a long and friendly association. Thereafter the members of both Societies dined together. The match and the dinner which followed it have been duly noted in the records of each Society.

The moralist will find ample food for thought therein, for the Burgess account of the event in its *Chronicle* makes no mention of defeat, and the Bruntsfield Minute, reproduced in Clark's *Golf*, makes no mention of the fact that at the dinner Captain Duncan of the Burgess was in the Chair 'as head of the senior club.'

Foundation Dates

That statement deserves respectful consideration. The seniority thus stated in the Burgess *Chronicle* version of events echoes an earlier entry in a Bruntsfield minute book, of 25 April 1818, which is about a preliminary meeting of a joint committee representing Burgess and Bruntsfield golfers, 'for cementing more firmly that friendship which ought ever to subsist among golfers' and to make arrangements for the match and dinner: Captain Duncan was to take the Chair, 'he being Captain of the senior Club', and Captain Gardner was to act as croupier.

This admission it would be unworthy to deny, but the extent of the seniority is another matter, for it depends upon assertions of foundation dates and they are notoriously unreliable for all organisations seeking to establish a respectable antiquity. Guide-books for medieval abbeys, for instance, invariably start by stating with complacent finality that the abbey was founded in 1128, or whatever, when the said date is a vast over-simplification of what could be and usually was a prolonged process of original suggestions, declarations of intent, discussions, and final decisions. To any one of those happenings a formal foundation date might eventually be attached. Historically, it is little more than an indicator, a peg to hang a History upon.

The Burgess indicator is a strong one, and has been cogently argued by Mr Cameron Robbie in his Burgess *Chronicle*. The Bruntsfield indicator is also a strong one, derived from a minute quoted by Clark in his *Golf*. Place-dated Bruntsfield Links, 30 July 1790, it reads:

> As this Golfing Society had subsisted above thirty years, a proposal had been some time ago made for having an Uniform. Mr A. Brown produced a design viz. two clubs crossed with four balls, with the opposite [sic] motto below – Inde Salus.

This was considered and approved by the Meeting. Almost two years before, Mr Brown had 'presented the Arms of the Society blazoned thus—Vert two Golf Clubs in Saltyr, their Heads in chief proper between four Golf Balls Argent. Motto in an escroll above the shield, *Inde Salus*', [which being translated means, 'thus, hence, in this way, is good health']

This is unequivocal, powerful evidence that the accepted foundation date of independent existence is wrong and must be earlier than 1760, and likely to be between 1745 and 1760.

When the Bruntsfield proposal was thus recorded Burgess was similarly moved to be uniformed and badged, 'as is universally done by other Societies of golfers'. To be sure there were not many which might have done, but the coincidence of those two decisions is further evidence of 'the cordiality and good understanding which subsisted betwixt the two clubs'.

The Bruntsfield golfers were ever alert to preserve the amenities of the Links, which they had for ever been taught to believe was held sacred for the healthful exercise of golf, and they were active in protest against recurrent threats to them. Quarrying, roadworks, military activities, and even a canal, by Rennie, which would have come along the avenue of Melville Drive and cut across the Links obliquely NE – SW to converge upon the south end of Wright's Houses, detaching the Golf Tavern from the Links thereby, exemplify unavoidable interruptions and dire possibilities. As dutiful and zealous guardians of their privileges they banded together in January 1791 and under the nominal leadership of the Burgess addressed a Memorial to the Provost, Magistrates and Council of the City which courteously and convincingly argued against a proposal to make a new road in front of the Golf Tavern, between it and the links, thus anticipating the abortive threat of Rennie's canal some twenty years later.

The proposal and the golfers' reaction to it make good reading. The proposers made an eloquent plea for this better road, in the following terms: '*The Trustees now after the fullest investigation propose that the present narrow Lane or Road lying between the Wrights houses and Burntsfield (sic) Links shall be widened . . . The Ground to be taken off the links will be very inconsiderable and be very well spared without incommodating the Golfers . . .*', and they go on to allege '*the narrow, dirty and confined approaches to the City from the South, a prodigious increase in wheeled vehicles, machines, obstructions, nastiness and accidents*'. And they furthermore declare frequent travellers' complaints about '*the worst and most inconvenient of all Entries into Edinbr which must always be the case while it is carried thro' so narrow and dirty a village inhabited by so many low people*'. The Magistrates having considered these damaging assertions, and having also visited the ground, found for the opposition nonetheless, being of the opinion that 'on account of the health of the inhabitants, the Links so near the City ought to be preserved'. The next year, in June 1792, and very probably not unconnected with the golfers' success in resisting a proposal to make a new road up the east side of Wrights Houses, they subscribed 10/6 each towards a subscription for the Lord Provost and Magistrates for the expense of making one up the west side, for the purpose of preserving the Links entire; this alternative road being the present Bruntsfield Place.

Apart from such disturbances at Bruntsfield Links the peace of the golfers was upset by the ways of the military and the concern of the Town Council with flying golf balls and public safety. Indeed, as we have noted, the Bruntsfield Allied undertook to pay for broken street lamps, presumably those broken by their own play. The military too posed problems after 1797, especially after 1803 when the Peace of Amiens expired and the threat of imminent invasion was heady. All men were soldiers, ready to repel the footsteps of invaders rude, as Walter Scott put it, and he was in his warlike element. Anti-Napoleonic fervour was aflame and Edinburgh became an armed camp. Thinking men were in a great and general fright, 'which increased in proportion as they thought', as Lord Cockburn relates in his

Memorials. And this model of forensic eloquence commanded eighty privates including the King's Physician, Dr Gregory (inventor of the Mixture), two officers, four sergeants, corporals, and a trumpeter, 'all of whom trembled (or at least were bound to tremble) when I spoke'. Professors, lecturers, doctors, douce citizens, wheeled and stood-at-ease in the Quad of the Old College. Bench and Bar carried side-arms as well as golf clubs destined for Muirfield some day, and among these gentlemen-at-arms none paraded more fervently and galloped with greater ardour than Walter Scott, founder, quartermaster and secretary of the Royal Edinburgh Light Dragoons, upon his charger 'Lenore'.

As early as 1799 the Town Council agreed to a proposal to level the links east of Wrights Houses 'equal to the manoeuvring of a thousand men and more'. Some years later, when the fever of war was somewhat cooler, the Gordon Highlanders, stationed at the Castle and exercising on the Links, were forced to capitulate to a Bruntsfield golfer, one Stein, who demonstrated his convictions and resentment by driving his ball, rather badly but with awful deliberation, into their ranks, and thereafter breaking his club across the shoulders of the luckless and probably non-golfing Gordon who had been foolish enough to pick it up and throw it aside. The episode caused much trouble, for the heroic Stein refused to apologise for it, maintaining that the Gordons ought not to have been there at all. We may add in parenthesis that such a confrontation did not occur at the old Kilspindie Club, where the whizzing of the Volunteers' bullets constituted an unwelcome hazard, whereupon the Kilspindie members retreated to Gullane, where they were not welcomed, and then perforce formed the Old Luffness Club in 1867, on the links opposite Luffness House, and played on a green laid out at their behest by Old Tom Morris and Mr Hope, the Laird of Luffness. It was for this course, now superseded, that Bruntsfield demonstrated its East Lothian sympathies, of which more later, with a contribution towards the repair of its Peffer Bridge.

Little is known about the details of early play at Bruntsfield, but the significant minute of 1790, to which reference has been made regarding the age of the Society, proves that golf was long established there at that time, and was sufficiently well ordered to require a uniform to be worn at play, even without a Captain to wear it. In fact Captains were not thought of in any formal sense until 1793, when it was proposed that for the good regulation of the Society a Captain should be chosen annually and have a caddie to attend him, clothed at the expense of the Society. Not another Captain is recorded until 1799. But caddies insist on recognition. Essentially they were carriers, for instance Edinburgh 'water-cadies' carried kegs of water from street pumps to private houses, until water was piped from the Pentland Hills. Generally useful as messengers they were by a city ordinance of 1739 regulated and badged. But, more important to our purpose, they have ever been a part of golf. They figure conspicuously in all early pictures, prints, paintings, photographs too, of golfing occasions large and small, including Bruntsfield Links in the eighteenth century (Plate 3).

In the depression following the end of the Napoleonic War in 1815 labouring work was awarded to the needy, among whom starving weavers from the west of Scotland were employed in making roads round the Calton Hill and Salisbury Crags, a feature which was popularised by Scott in *The Heart of Midlothian* before gunpowder and pick-axe had done grievous harm. (Some were suspected of radical tendencies, hence the 'Radical Road'). At the same time Bruntsfield Links was cleared of whins and abandoned quarries. During the Parliamentary debates on the Edinburgh Improvement Bill of 1827, which saved the south side of Princes Street from builders and developers, the Meadows and the Links were likewise saved from building, much to the additional displeasure of the Town Council for the loss of immensely valuable building land which they perforce had to agree to because the Bill would otherwise have been lost, as Professor Youngson explains in *The Making of Classical Edinburgh*. It was perhaps as a consequence of this interest in the Links as a rural asset that many of Bruntsfield's fine trees, remnants of the ancient oak forest of the Burgh Muir which provided the Old Town with the material for its half-timbered houses, were also saved. And there were many trees (Plates 2 and 3), as the following account amply testifies.

Notwithstanding the arrival of cholera in January and the death of Sir Walter Scott in September, the great event of 1832 was the passing of the Reform Act and the monster but orderly procession of the Trades in celebration of the triumph. 'There was not only no rioting' wrote Cockburn, 'but scarcely even disrespect.' But there might have been a bad moment or two at Bruntsfield all the same, for had the Iron Duke not said that in the event of trouble he would tranquillise the country in three days? However, the Scottish crowds were quiet, although rejoicing, and when 15,000 assembled at Bruntsfield Links (*The Scotsman* of the day says 80,000, which probably includes 30–40,000 spectators as well, for the Links are reported to have been full and hustings were erected along the north side) the trees were festooned with urchins. When the procession moved off it vividly and tumultuously represented trades of all descriptions, such as those so comprehensively represented in Wright's Houses. With bands playing and flags waving the exuberant throng processed through the city as far as the boundary of Leith, then a separate Burgh, where a man could sleep with his head in Leith and his feet in Edinburgh and drink in a bar with different opening hours at each end.

In the absence of sound evidence one cannot particularise much about play at Bruntsfield, but it was good enough in all respects to attract James McEwan in 1770. Founder of the renowned clubmaking family whose work, it is worth saying in passing, was stamped with a thistle motif and is greatly valued, he was succeeded at Bruntsfield by Peter McEwan who was considered in 1819 to be a very fit person to be an officer to the Bruntsfield and to be provided with a uniform and badge accordingly. In 1780 James McEwan was joined by Douglas Gourlay, a feather-ball maker of good repute. In a Bruntsfield minute of 1820, at a time when club competitions were invariably for prize balls (the hope of winning golf balls, costly items in feathery days, was one reason for joining a club), it was proposed that in future Prize Balls should be 'Gourlays'. The McEwans and the Gourlays resided in Wright's Houses and together established a workshop at Bruntsfield which supplied clubs and balls throughout the golfing world of the time, which was the east coast of Scotland with satellites at Blackheath and Westward Ho! But, a sign of the times, in the 1840s they transferred their allegiance to Musselburgh, although continuing to be represented at Bruntsfield, in evidence of which the Society has in its possession many receipts and other papers relating to them: a telling example is a series of receipts from McEwan for an annual payment of a guinea for the making of holes at Bruntsfield Links, beginning in 1863 and sent from 36 Wright's Houses. Commercially there are many receipted accounts for the purchase of golf balls supplied by McEwan, Gourlay, and Brown of St Andrews ('Croquet, Billiards, Cricket Bats, balls and Leg Guards, Tubular gloves, Billiard Cues made to Order, Golf Clubs carefully repaired'), also '12 doz. best golf balls @ 10/- for £6, St Andrews July 1864').

A memorable and historic receipt, on a scrap of paper, which the Society is happy to possess, is from Old Tom Morris to Robert Chambers, jnr., the young Bruntsfield golfer who won what we may call the proto-Amateur Championship at St Andrews in 1858, not then a recurring event, the 'Amateur' of today not being initiated until 1885. Morris's receipt is for payment of 4 doz. golf balls for £2, and it is signed Thomas Morris. It is also glossed 'pd. by James Williamson of Burgess Club Sept. 8/65', a friendly act. But nevertheless Chambers was a Bruntsfield man when he won that Championship at the age of 20.

And we must admire a splendid letter from Douglas McEwan. It shows that however much the Links of Musselburgh was increasingly attractive to golfers at Edinburgh and at Leith, the Links of Bruntsfield was still a force to be reckoned with, and so was its clubmaker. The letter is addressed to Thos. S. Aitchison, originator of the *Reminiscences*, ('so full of good-humoured fun that he was the friend of everyone'). It is penned by another but signed Douglas McEwan, in a very shaky hand, and it reads thus in the most splendid English:

> Bruntsfield Links
> Edin. 8 Nov. 1864
> Thos. S. Aitchison. Esq.
>
> Sir,
> I have received yours of the 7th enclosing P.O. order for £1.11/- for which I thank you. I notice with regret, your complaint of the way the duties you refer to have been discharged.
>
> I may state in explanation of the want of flags last Saturday, that there are none left to put out.
>
> About 2 months ago I supplied a set at my own expense, costing 12/- and 3 of them were stolen from the Links in one day.
>
> The only way by which the inconvenience you refer to can be remedied, is by having a new set of flags provided—as the Burgess, Warrender, Allied and Merchiston Clubs have each furnished a set—while the Bruntsfield have never done so I expect that they will take their turn—and supply a set, or give me an order to do so at their expense.
>
> I am
> sir
> Your Obedt. Servt.
> Douglas McEwan

Much must needs be inferred from the recorded actions of the Bruntsfield golfing societies in their endeavours to protect the links from actions injurious to the chief duty of man, but reliable information on the details of matches is lacking on the whole, and in the absence of reliable documentary evidence we must admit defeat. An important event concerning Bruntsfield and the Burgess admits of no doubt at all however. The Burgess *Chronicle* states categorically that 'the first match between Edinburgh Burgess Golfing Society and the Bruntsfield Links Golf Club took place at Bruntsfield in 1803'. The facts of the matter are not recorded but the ensuing dinner is, by Bruntsfield, which says characteristically that the evening was spent with great harmony and some fine songs. Bruntsfield was never wrapped in dismal thinkings.

The encounter was not renewed for some fourteen years, however, not until the previously mentioned occasion in 1818 when Captain Duncan of Burgess took the chair at the customary dinner after the match. In 1819 the match was repeated. It then lapsed until 1853, when Bruntsfield proposed a resumption and a trophy for the two societies to contend annually. The trophy was made, and it inaugurated a long series of fixtures, mostly played at Bruntsfield, but also at Musselburgh, Leith, Gullane, and North Berwick. Between 1880 and 1886 there was a lapse, and the trophy then being in the possession of the Burgess it remained there by default. It is with the Burgess still, and is no longer in contention, but a replica is played for by the Councils of the two Societies to this day.

For a hundred years and more the Society was domiciled at Bruntsfield. Latterly at least it is known to have had a certain fixed routine, Bruntsfield Links on Saturdays at 2 o'clock, Musselburgh Links on Tuesdays with the 11.20 from Waverley in winter, after 4 o'clock in summer, for the Society's regular meetings. Play at Bruntsfield, in fact, was much affected by time-tables, even calendars, for inland courses crossed common land given over to pasturage in the summer months when the grass was greener and longer. Golf was restricted on the whole to a couple of months in Spring and three in Autumn. There was little play in August and September, and when resumed in October the green was at its worst. An attempt was made to improve the putting greens by importing sand from Musselburgh and spreading it upon them, but the grazing tenant promptly objected and the costly attempt failed. We shall return to the vexing question of pasturage when we come to consider work and play at Barnton but with regard to the more immediate question of pasturage at Bruntsfield Links a minute of the Society in July 1852 is surely significant. It was then agreed by the Council that on 25 September there should be prizes of six, four and two 'gutta perchas': a decision in July anticipates play at the end of September. There was none of consequence in between.

This incidentally is the first Bruntsfield mention of the 'gutta percha'. This new solid ball which superseded the 'feathery', at St Andrews in 1848, was durable, cost half as much, and brought golf to the people. But it was dark, even black, could not take paint, and was much lost. Caddies had perforce to carry at least a half dozen spares to add to their load of wet sand or clay for tees. Caddies have always been among the heavy laden.

During the Society's long life at Bruntsfield many prizes, as well as the inexhaustible golf balls, were played for, but they were ephemeral distinctions, non-recurring rewards for a day's success. The practice of offering such *ad hoc* prizes as personal contributions to the Society's competitions—ink-stands, a drawing-room lamp, a set of the Waverley novels, a set of golf clubs—did indeed continue until recent times, but the only prizes, or more properly the only permanent and established trophies, were the Gold Medal, the Society's oldest of 1819, and most prestigious, which had to be played for in uniform, and the Cairns Medal of 1839, which was presented by the retiring Captain

1. The Clubhouse of 1898 from the 18th, and later alterations. The rounded window wrapped round an original corner and the lower accommodation on the right has been superseded by that illustrated on Plate 21.

2. Golfers at work on Bruntsfield Links, from an engraving of 1798. A colour version of this hangs in the Hall of the Clubhouse, by Slack, dated 1797. Note the early clubs, the dense and abundant trees, St Giles crown spire on the right. The diminutive building at the far left of the castle rock was succeeded in the late 19th century by the high block which overlooks the west end of Princes Street and gardens today

3. 'Edinburgh Castle from Bruntsfield Links', by J. Ewbank, RSA. (1799–1847) Golf at Bruntsfield Links in the late 18th century. Note the figure in right middle-ground, a caddie with his bundle of clubs, and centre middle-ground a player about to play. The massive Barrack block, on left, 1798. Again, the artist's attention has been waylaid by the trees and the golfers, but the picture is really about the view to the Castle. It also hangs in the Hall of the Clubhouse.

4. The Golf Hotel, 17th century, first home of the Burgess golfers at Bruntsfield. Painted board. Between the words two clubs crossed, with three balls. Reproduced with permission from the Burgess *Chronicle* where it is captioned 'Golf Tavern Bruntsfield Links. Characteristic 17th cent. domestic architecture, steep pitched roof, raised doorway, harled walls'. Note player with bundle of clubs.

5. The 'Golf Hotel' on the left: the large block on the right is the tenement containing 30 Wright's Houses where the Bruntsfield Society had their being 'in a house facing the Links, close to the old Golf Tavern which formed the headquarters of the Burgess Golf Club'. The old 'Golf Hotel' has been demolished, 30 Wright's Houses was in the 'Golf Tavern' of today. The wayward uses of the words 'Hotel' and 'Tavern' have caused some confusion.

6. The 'Golf Tavern' of today, in Barclay Terrace, Wright's Houses, overlooking the Links. Originally a late-eighteenth/early-nineteenth century tenement with several rooms, or dwellings, one of which, '30 Wright's Houses', was the Bruntsfield Society's Clubhouse. At the extreme right, in shadow, is the door to the outside stair to first and second floor accommodation. Up this many a Bruntsfield Society golfer must have wended his eager or weary way. The building was converted in 1899 to its present appearance, with contemporary interior, by R.M. Cameron, who had designed the Burgess Clubhouse at Barnton three years before.

7. Detail of pl.5. Bruntsfield Society's old Clubhouse, now the 'Golf Tavern'. Note the outside stair to upper accommodation and clubroom. Reproduced from Aitchison and Lorimer's *Reminiscences*.

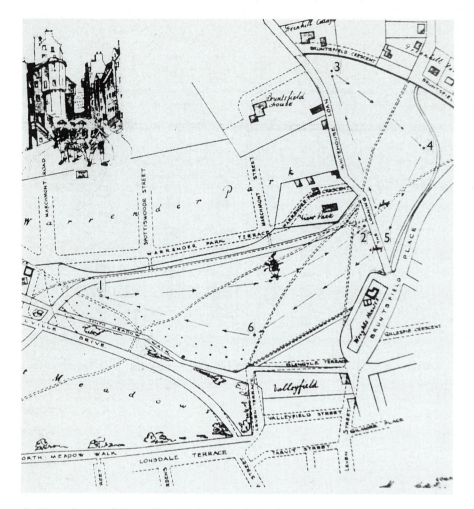

8. Map of part of Bruntsfield Links with the early course and holes superimposed. Alongside Bruntsfield Place is Wright's Houses with the old Golf Hotel clearly shown. Here Burgess met. But not shown is Bruntsfield's neighbouring Clubhouse, in 30 Wright's Houses, a domestic tenement among others which occupied the rest of this 'island' site.

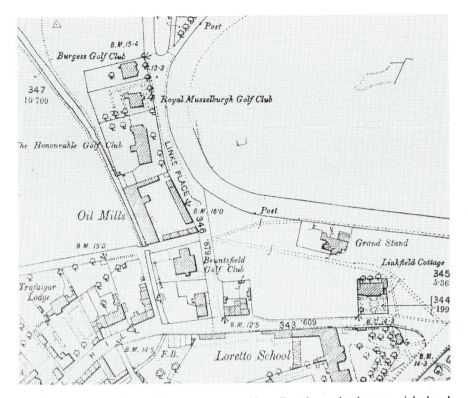

9. The main road from Edinburgh leaves Musselburgh at the bottom right-hand corner of this map, and bends right to run alongside the Race-Course for a half mile or so. A turn round Loretto School corner quickly brings the golfwise traveller to the road-end of the most historical street in the golfing world, where four of the world's oldest clubs built their Musselburgh Clubhouses, looking down the Links. The empty area at the top of the map is the west end of the long oval of the famous Musselburgh Links, where six 'Opens' were played. It has been enclosed by a Race-Course since c.1816, when the Grand Stand was built, to be enlarged 1886, to the detriment of Bruntsfield's brand-new Clubhouse no doubt. In order of appearance, with historical dates, Bruntsfield (1760) Hon. Co (1744), Royal Musselburgh (1774), Burgess (1735): all 19th cent. buildings, new Clubhouses for old clubs.

10. Musselburgh Links. This postcard of Links Place, c.1900, was produced before the Race-Course Grandstand was extended in 1886. It shows from left to right the old grandstand of 1816, Bruntsfield Clubhouse, the old Seamill, the Honourable Company's Clubhouse, then the Royal Musselburgh and, disappearing off right, the Burgess Clubhouse.

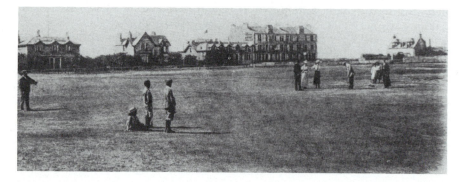

11. Links Place, continued. Honourable Company, Musselburgh, Burgess. Note in this and no.9, the flag-poles at each Clubhouse.

12. The Musselburgh Clubhouse, opened May 1886, quit October 1897, and became the Social Club of the Brunton Wire Works, which it still is.

13. Musselburgh Race Day, a postcard of c.1900. This is real, not 'an artist's impression'. Probably one reason for the golfer's return to Edinburgh. This photograph might well have been taken from the Clubhouse. Note the vehicles parked just in front of it.

14. Detail of no.12. Crossed clubs, three balls and a thistle (as used in contemporary stationery of the Society).

15. Another window-head, with BLGC monogram. Very good sculptured and plain masonry. The workmanship and design, the detailing, scale, and the first-class masonwork of this work at Musselburgh recalls the entrance-way at the present Clubhouse, which must be of Musselburgh parentage.

By the la' Harry
Thus shall not go for Nothing

16. From Kay's *Portraits*, Alexander McKellar, the 'Cock o' the Green', a memorable figure on Bruntsfield Links. At the behest of Douglas Gourlay and Peter McEwan, Kay drew this caricature in 1803; drawn on the Links in full pursuit of his renowned, ridiculed and compulsive passion. Picture here reproduced to illustrate the long shafted, long headed clubs and the inevitable closed stance.

17. The Gold Medal. The Society's oldest, 1819.

18. The Cairns Medal, originally for play at Musselburgh, 1839.

19. Old clubs and balls in the Clubhouse.

20. A further selection of old clubs and balls in the Clubhouse.

21. The Clubhouse today, behind the 18th. (flag on left).

Cairns before he resigned office in that year. It was expressly intended for play at Musselburgh.

Play at Musselburgh was no new idea, not even in 1839. For years the members had been going there, where the links were open for play all the year round and pleased golfers when Bruntsfield could not. Contrariwise, there was a strong Musselburgh presence at Bruntsfield. The McEwans and the Gourlays lived in Wright's Houses. So did George Robertson, ballmaker, but in 1831 he too moved to Musselburgh and resided in Mill Hill, probably in Mrs Taylor's boarding house where many another ballmaker and clubmaker is to be found. In their *Reminiscences* Aitchison and Lorimer recall that it was the custom of the Bruntsfield Society to rent a 'box' [locker] from John Gourlay, of the renowned family—a golfer himself, ballmaker, tenant of the Grand Stand and Supervisor of the races. His house in Mill Hill was by way of being a golfing rendezvous. Players foregathered there, as did hopeful and expectant caddies.

The emigrant Bruntsfield golfers did in fact do more than merely rent a box. At least from 1862, which is the date of our earliest surviving paper, they yearly rented a 'clubroom' from him in his 'Golf House', Musselburgh, for £8 invariably, this rent being duly receipted at that address with other items such as '4 doz. golf balls £2–8/-'. There is no description nor detailed evidence of life at 'Golf House, Musselburgh' but other bills and occasional papers testify to a known and respectable existence there until 1869, the year of Gourlay's death and the acquisition of St Peter's Episcopal Church, which was comprehensively converted to make a home-from-home which the clubroom in Gourlay's 'Golf House' never could have been.

Therein resided the problem. There was inevitably growing dissatisfaction with conditions at Bruntsfield. There was congestion and a mounting concern of the Town Council about all things golfwise, which was opposed by the golfers and led to the Town's purchase in 1889 of the Braid Hills as an alternative site (the name is not derived from James Braid of the 'Great Triumvirate', Vardon, Braid and Taylor, but from the Gaelic for 'upland'). So, by mid-century the ever-increasing flights from Bruntsfield to Musselburgh had the Bruntsfield members in a quandary. While the Bruntsfield Links' star was sinking Musselburgh's was rising, at its zenith in the 1870s, when, for a brief period before decline in favour of St Andrews, it was the Home of Golf.

The dilemma which confronted the Bruntsfield members was inevitably influenced by an increasing imbalance of membership, movingly and sensibly related in the last chapter of *Reminiscences*. The older members held strongly to their loyalty but admitted it was really a case of bowing to the inevitable.

'*With all its discomforts and poor accommodation we were very fond of our little house at Bruntsfield, while the green, bad as it was, was never crowded. Our debate, however, ended as it was bound to end, in our recognising the fact that at no distant date we should have no choice in the matter, and that it would be better to yield gracefully at once; and this was accordingly done.*'

The magnanimity of this acknowledgment, its good nature, brings to mind many a telling phrase in the published minutes of the Society which might otherwise be thought trivial, such as: 'the evening was spent with more than stereotyped happiness, harmony and hilarity', . . . 'the meeting as usual cracked their jokes over a glass and enjoyed the evening harmoniously with a song' . . . 'the evening spent with great harmony, and some fine songs' . . . 'The Captain, Mr Kirkhope, and Mr A.W. Usher entertained the company with a song'. And when Captain Aitchison led his team to Leven, there to play the King James VI Club of Perth, and they all arrived the night before and dined together, characteristically he invited 'our opponents to commence the harmony by giving us a song'. But none would, or couldn't. 'I remember being quite proud of my team. I began with my right hand man, and every one of the Bruntsfield without exception sang a song'. The Bruntsfield songsters were something to be proud of. But next day, he confesses, we were not equally successful on the green.

The Bruntsfield Clubhouse of diminishing importance presented itself as a problem to its seventy members who played at Bruntsfield and at Musselburgh too and were averse to the increasing of membership as a way of raising funds for the building of another clubhouse at Musselburgh. To abandon Bruntsfield altogether was never considered. Instead, St Peter's Episcopal Chapel in Mill Hill presented itself as a solution.

CHAPTER 2

The Move to Musselburgh

St Peter's Episcopal Chapel was built in 1784 on a site now covered by a housing scheme, more or less opposite the historic and surviving Golf Tavern. Nothing remains of the church nor the adjacent ecclesiastical establishment which it served. It was a typical small eighteenth-century church; without side aisles. A central aisle opened into an apse at the east end. This accommodated the altar: to the north of the apse—the font, to the south a double-decker pulpit. The long central aisle served rows of pews on each side, with a special laird's pew in front. The windows were round-headed. However, Episcopal stipends being miserably low, the incumbent in 1825 began to take in pupils, and in 1829 he purchased Loretto House from Sir John Hope. Thus Loretto School came into being. In 1869 it was decided to build a new church with the proceeds of the sale of the old. Thus a Bruntsfield Musselburgh clubhouse came into being, conveniently near the Links at the east end of the town.

A clubmaster's house and suitable domestic appointments were added or altered to the church and great was the work thereat, as innumerable accounts and receipts testify, from tradesmen in Musselburgh and Fisherrow, for structural repairs and modifications, and for household items of all kinds and sizes from carpets to kitchen towels, bell-pulls, 67 brass coat hooks, fitting up club boxes, clearing snow from flat roof and repairing damage caused by recent storms. While all this was going on in 1868/70, and indeed during the immediately preceding years in Gourlay's 'Golf House', the Bruntsfield Links connection survived and was unaffected. Golf was still played there regularly and competitively, formal meetings and occasional dinners continued to be held there and Mrs Stewart was still the housekeeper. Rates and Taxes prolonged the exactions of authority however and to the growing dissatisfaction with the playing conditions of the Bruntsfield green there was increasing hesitation and doubt about the cost of running two clubhouses when interest in one was diminishing. In 1876 the Musselburgh connection was fortified when members were sounded as to their prejudices and convictions and a test vote was taken. Sixteen voted for a total move to Musselburgh, eleven voted against it. Later that year the Council decided that the Society's financial statement should be exhibited in both clubhouses and in the same month it attempted, unsuccessfully, to sell off the whole property at Bruntsfield Links. Only the Warrender Club declared an interest and that was unacceptable.

In January 1878 the Council formally decided to discontinue the clubhouse at Bruntsfield. Three months later the vexing question of what to do with it was satisfactorily resolved. For himself and friends Mr A. Usher, a former Captain, rented the street and lower flats, bought thirteen boxes and much of the furniture and undertook the restoration, painting and papering necessary after the removal of boxes to Musselburgh (presumably those which he did not require), all as sitting tenants. Mrs Stewart continued to occupy the rest of the house. The continuators at Bruntsfield, familiarly known as 'The Club', agreed to allow the departed the use of a room for general and council meetings. In fact, the house at Bruntsfield continued to be the headquarters and true home of the Society, even if only a faithful remnant was there to prove it. The 'allowance' which the Bruntsfield Society paid to 'The Club' for the use of the room was reduced in 1881 because of the very occasional benefit derived by it, but the allowance continue to be paid nevertheless, until 1890 no less, by which time the Society had left what used to be St Peter's Chapel and had been in occupation of a new-built clubhouse for four years.

The unequivocal allegiance of the Bruntsfield/Musselburgh golfers to their old home at Bruntsfield Links, when the growing momentum of a move to Musselburgh and the weight of conflicting loyalties might well have tilted exclusively towards Musselburgh, was a fact of fundamental importance in the Society's history, for it kept alive a real interest and practical connection with Bruntsfield, and it saved the name which might otherwise have withered.

In 1893 the house in Wright's Houses, which had been for so long the home of the Society, was converted to be the 'Golf Tavern' of today.

For the golfwise inquirer travelling from Edinburgh the far end of Musselburgh *mérite un détour*, as the Michelin map would say. Where the main road leaves the town and bends right to run alongside the racecourse and the golf links there is also a left-hand turn, round the corner of Loretto School (Plate 9). This is the end of Mill Hill (which is in fact quite flat). The road passes along the back of the racecourse grandstand and soon crosses the end of the most interesting golf road in the world. It is now called Balcarres Road in a modern street nameplate, but beside it, cut into the corner stone of a small block of houses, its early name still shows, 'Golf Place', and upon the lintel of the first doorway of this street there is a sculptured emblem of crossed clubs about a golf ball which bears the date 1886, much weathered. This is a significant date in Bruntsfield history. On 27 May 1886 the new-built BLGS clubhouse was opened and grand competitions for the Gold Medal, the Ladies

Cup, and the Morrison-Turnbull Cup were held over the adjacent links, and a grand dinner was held in the new Clubhouse afterwards. This clubhouse was the latest of a remarkable series in Golf Place (Plates 9, 10, 11).

The Four Clubhouses

There were four historic clubhouses in this short road which closed the links at the west end. In open land each was built isolated and separate to look down the length of the links to Mrs Forman's renowned inn which closed the links at the other end. The Honourable Company's was first, 1865, the Royal Musselburgh's next, 1873; the Burgess in 1875 and, finally, the Bruntsfield in 1886. The prestigious buildings are still there, in varying degrees of alteration and re-use. An old picture postcard, which must have been made about the turn of the century, shows the row of clubhouses as seen from the Links (Plate 10). The Honourable Company's has a row of four gabled outshots at ground floor level, running into a larger main block comprising ground and first-floor accommodation. The outshots, which seem to have had crow-stepped gable-ends, were built over at some later date to meet the wall-head level of the larger and higher block. In the surviving gable-ends of the former outshots there is a window whose sill projects beyond the wall-face and is carried by two projecting and moulded corbels, an unusual and interesting architectural detail which occurs upon the main block also and proves the contemporaneity of the two parts. The whole makes rather a large mass today, but the main walling still reveals the ghost of the four outshots which were over-built. The Honourable Company's clubhouse at Musselburgh Links became the Bodywise Fitness Club and the rooms of Masonic Lodge 112.

Next in order of appearance in the street is the clubhouse of the Royal Musselburgh, numbered 9 in the row (Plates 10 and 11). This is a villa-like house; in fact it is occupied as such today, but in the postcard a flag-pole reveals its clubhouse origins, as it does with the other buildings shown. Next came the Burgess, a very accomplished building by John C. Hay in 1875, with elaborate and highly distinctive detailing in the manner of Alexander 'Greek' Thompson, the eminent Glasgow architect of the mid-nineteenth century. This clubhouse became a restaurant when the Burgess left it in 1894 to return to Edinburgh. Its old Musselburgh clubhouse, doomed to become a restaurant, is now a dental laboratory, and consequently altered internally, but outside it is good and essentially unaltered, a fine example of superior late nineteenth-century domestic architecture. Of some archaeological interest is a large rectangular recess in the front wall, labelled 'Edenvale'. This housed a sculptured panel of golfers, by John Rhind, which is now in the external face of the east wall of the Burgess clubhouse at Barnton. Their clubhouse at Musselburgh is well worth a visit, even to view from outside, for it is no ordinary building. It has been extended in the same style at its north end.

Even more praiseworthy however is the Bruntsfield clubhouse of 1886. (Plate 12). It is now the social club of the Brunton Wire Works and consequently has been somewhat disturbed inside. But no harm has been done and outside it is complete and unaltered. It is on the whole a very remarkable example of superior domestic architecture of the period, by a prominent Edinburgh architect, Hippolyte J. Blanc. The Brunton name is honoured in Musselburgh even today, with the Brunton Memorial Hall of 1971 by Sir William Kininmouth, with gilded relief sculpture by Tom Whalen prominently confronting the street, a major civic enterprise. The Brunton Wire Works Social Club is worthy of note as occupant of a true Bruntsfield Clubhouse, and no less important and interesting is the fact that the company took over the old Seamill nearby (hence Mill Hill) in 1901, for the manufacture of piano wire, then a German monopoly. Eventually Brunton's steel wire was famous. It rigged First World War biplanes, airships, the R34 and the R100, designed by Barnes Wallis. It was the only company in Britain which manufactured this essential aircraft component.

The Bruntsfield Clubhouse at Musselburgh Links is still there and in good shape (Plates 12, 14, 15). Alone of the four Clubhouses of historic lineage in the street it is the only one which displays its golf origins. A great bow window, plainly not that of an ordinary dwelling, overlooks the links with an uninterrupted view eastwards over the whole length of the green to Mrs Forman's inn. Where it is it could not be anything else but a golf clubhouse, one feels, but, in addition, it displays unequivocally its Bruntsfield parentage. Two three-light mullioned and transomed windows carry sculptured pediments over the lintels. One contains 'BLGS' in a cartouche nicely panelled, within a semicircular arch, the other has a moulded panel with crossed clubs and three balls, and instead of the usual fourth, a thistle, being a variation of the Society's heraldic devices occurring also on the official stationery of the period. The fine detailing of these features at the Musselburgh clubhouse, and the mouldings thereof ('You can judge a civilisation by its mouldings'), may be seen at the entrance doorway of the present Clubhouse at Davidsons Mains

There is something disconcerting about this splendid and imposing doorway however. It does not seem to belong. The masonry joints do not inspire confidence, the top member of the cornice has been trimmed to fit the corner, and the scale and detail of the whole is foreign to the plain-spoken early Clubhouse which it enters. It looks like a rebuild, an insertion, an importation from Musselburgh perhaps? But the detail within the tympanum is twice dated—1761 and 1898. This distances the work from the Musselburgh Clubhouse to which it might belong but does not. The date 1898 proclaims the new Barnton Gate Clubhouse, although the workmanship speaks of Musselburgh.

Nothing else in the doorway's quasi-Renaissance style is to be found elsewhere in the plain and unadorned Clubhouse of architect-member Taylor, but much of it is to be found in its Musselburgh predecessor by architect-member Blanc. The doorway is an alien feature in a new Clubhouse of good but simple design requiring no ornament, but it presents itself as a problem requiring explanation. Lacking evidence of the architect's brief, and working drawings, we must resort to guesswork to reconcile the Musselburgh style with the Barnton date, and it is suggested, merely, for it is an alien thing, that this doorway was designed and made in Musselburgh, by those who made the Musselburgh Clubhouse, for use in Edinburgh, to gratify Bruntsfield's instinctive feeling for continuity, already evident at Bruntsfield and Musselburgh, to include in the new Clubhouse a thought of the old.

This explanation, fanciful though it might seem to be, is entirely consistent with Bruntsfield thinking in the past and particularly in this year, when Incorporation was in the air and the membership had formally to be disbanded in order to rejoin *ab initio*. In a conscious attempt to maintain continuity members of the 'old' Society were given due and adequate notice of the impending constitutional reform, with sufficient time to become members of the 'new', Incorporate, Society.

Play and Players at Musselburgh

The Links at Musselburgh was originally of four holes only, increased to seven, achieved eight in 1838, and a full nine in 1870, when it was at its greatest, a Championship green, the venue for six 'Opens'. Today it is much curtailed by the racecourse and disturbed thereby, by that and other causes, but it is still playable, and one can follow the original first four holes straight to Mrs Forman's inn, an ancient hostelry on the Great North Road, well worth a visit for its golf relics and other consolations. Originally the Inn had a window in its west gable, still remembered, which overlooked the course and acted as a buffet hatch for golfers on the fourth green, where they 'recreated their fatigated corps'. 'A very worthy woman was Mrs Forman, and a great favourite. There was no fault to be found either with her whisky or her bottled beer and stout any more than with her bread and cheese, while the freshness of her eggs was the subject of universal encomium.'

A 'round' was not defined until 1858, when the R & A declared it to be of eighteen holes, 'unless otherwise stipulated'. Shorter courses, or greens, were then obliged to tailor their rounds accordingly, three times six holes at Bruntsfield Links, two times nine at Musselburgh, after 1870. And there was more to a course record than the number of strokes taken. Captain Bloxsom of Bruntsfield (Captain 1884–5), a man charged with a powerful voltage, was prominent in the building of the Musselburgh Clubhouse and won the Gold Medal on its opening in 1886. He broke a Musselburgh record in 1872 with 16 rounds of the nine-hole course, non-stop more or less between 6 a.m. and 9 p.m., his renowned caddy Johnny ('Fiery') Carey (Frontispiece), going on strike at the fourteenth. Furthermore, the minutes of the Aberdeen Golf Club record Bloxsom's remorseless energy in a similar episode in Aberdeenshire in July 1875. In fulfilment of an after-dinner undertaking to play 12 rounds and walk 10 miles in 24 hours he began at 6 a.m. and finished before 9 p.m. and thus he did his rounds: and thereafter he did his walk, and completed his task with hours to spare, keeping up his strength with a little solid food in small quantities every three or four hours, and copious libations of Liebig's Extract of Meat in a liquid state, as the Rev. John Kerr relates under 'Feats of Endurance'.

Bruntsfield golfers featured conspicuously in East Lothian golf, even before they opened their Musselburgh Clubhouse in 1886. The East Lothian Club had a strong Bruntsfield interest, Aitchison was an original member in 1859, and the names of Bloxsam, Usher, Paxton, Clapperton (W.R.), are distinguished in a strong Bruntsfield representation therein. Moreover, Clapperton was a founder-member and Preses of the Gullane Golf Club, its Captain 1882–4. Bloxsam was a member of it and of the Old Luffness Club whose origins we have mentioned (p. 18). He was moreover a tower of strength and Secretary of the Tantallon Club of North Berwick which voted thanks for his gratuitous services and declared that all credit was due to him for the high position it had attained. He was Secretary and Treasurer of the exclusive Roundell Club which featured conspicuously on Gullane Hill, and in 1884, when Captain of Bruntsfield, he won the Moncrieff Gold Medal of North Berwick New. W. Paxton (Captain 1886), a Monk of St Giles, was secretary and founder of the 'Gullane Golfers', a prestigious social club. A man of character, as indeed they all were, he went blind in 1892, but even so followed a foursome at Machrihanish, as Kerr records.

W.R. Clapperton, (Capt. 1868), was 'Imperator' of the Hankey-Pankey golfers, mostly Bruntsfield members seeking play on the links at Gullane. Although in their genial and wayward way the Hankey-Pankeys inherited golfward tendencies and were subservient to golf, they owned no rules nor anything so commonplace as a Captain, but pledged themselves to an 'Imperator' whose sceptre of office was a golf-club. The members were admitted by invitation and membership was a tribute, a testimony of taste and character. It began around 1870, was revived in 1981 when its trophy was discovered under the stairs in Gullane's Clubhouse.

For all East Lothian occasions in the 60s and 70s Bruntsfield golfers went by train or 'in an omnibus with four horses'. In 1871 the first horse-tram made its appearance, when the Bruntsfield Society was settling down at Musselburgh, wherefrom they continued to play at large, especially in East Lothian. Meetings at North Berwick are recorded, but as far as we can see no mention of its Bass Rock Club, which might be regretted, because its officials too had minds of their own and were not afraid to express them. Its Secretary and Treasurer resigned in 1879 as his conscience would not allow him to act with a body of men who held their meetings in public houses.

Fixtures were played off at Luffness, North Berwick and Gullane, but the Gold Medal, the Ladies' Cup and the Cairns Medal continued to be Musselburgh events. Nonetheless, for all that it meant to the Society practically and incidentally and for all that the Bruntsfield golfers did for East Lothian golf, which cannot lightly be dismissed, the Musselburgh interlude did not last long in the Society's eventful history. In 1879, just some ten years after converting St Peter's Episcopal Chapel into a Clubhouse and making a caretaker's house therein, disturbed voices were raised once more, and not without reason. The thought of yet another move was more than a passing tremor. Whether or not to join forces with the Burgess in opposing a proposal to build a Candlework near its Clubhouse, which would be greatly injurious to the amenity of the green', was largely dependent upon a concensus of opinions about another burning question altogether, viz., whether or not to build a new Bruntsfield Clubhouse. The time, July 1879, was thought to provide a good opportunity for the acquisition of suitable land, and it was decided in November to advertise the present clubhouse, with interesting results, not immediately apparent.

In 1882 there was a unanimous desire to explore for a site for a new Club-house, and for the cost of building one. In 1884 the Committee of St Peter's School, having got wind of future prospects, made it known informally that it would consider paying £800 to acquire the property, however altered in form and function. In fact in 1885 the Clubhouse was sold, but not to the Episcopal

Church, which continued to be interested, nor to the University Golf Club which could not raise the money, but to Major-General Hope, for £500 and unglamorous conditions of proleptic significance: viz., the w.c.s, urinals, and lavatory were to be considered fixtures, and grates and gas-fittings were to be had at valuation. Evidently General Hope was mindful of the needs of the Episcopal School which had been established in 1871 shortly after Bruntsfield had moved into the old chapel it had converted. To this in the fulness of time he wished to install the School.

In the event a new Musselburgh Clubhouse was built, according to the design and plans of Hippolyte J. Blanc, on a site purchased for £600. The work, which was to cost no more than £1500, including fees, did in fact cost more and a fine building it turned out to be, as one can see today. The wonder of it is that the Society left it ten years later, to return to Edinburgh and build another. One thinks of Alice, who was advised to take a return ticket every time the train stopped.

While negotiating the sale of the Mill Hill (St Peter's) Clubhouse the Society had conducted its formal meetings in Edinburgh, in the Café Royal and in Dowell's Rooms, but it now had no home in Musselburgh, and Clubmaster Day, ball and club maker, was eventually instructed to move boxes from the St Peter's Clubhouse to the Grandstand of the racecourse where he had a postal address. It was an expedient previously enjoyed by the Honourable Company which had so used the previous grandstand as a transit camp after formally quitting Leith Links in 1836, to take the lead for many years at Musselburgh in organising co-operative protection of golfers' interests, care and maintenance of the Musselburgh green, and organising efforts to ensure that subversive proposals affecting it would be properly obstructed.

At this time of uncertainty, May 1885, when Blanc's plans were still being considered and a temporary tenancy in the grandstand seemed to be inevitable, Burgess extended the hand of friendship by cordially offering the use of their Clubhouse, and honorary membership. This 'cordial and spontaneous offer', as Captain Bloxsom expressed it, was gratefully accepted. Thus Bruntsfield members used the grandstand and socialised in the Burgess Clubhouse but a few yards away, while its new Clubhouse was being built nearby. (cf. Plate 9)

Walter Day's duties during the Society's residence in the St Peter's Clubhouse, as well as the normal, had an interesting Musselburgh requirement. He was entitled to charge each member one shilling for taking his clubs to and from Inveresk Station if on the same day, but if on different days then one shilling each journey. He was to charge nothing for taking clubs to the carrier or clubmaker. It being quite a walk from the station to the

Mill Hill (St Peter's) Clubhouse, where the Society then was, the additional duties imposed upon the clubmaster, even allowing him a fee and a handcart, are indicative of lesser tribulations endured by members after the Society had resolved to leave Bruntsfield Links, a decision which generated much heat at the time.

In 1879, just ten years after taking up residence in St Peter's Episcopal Chapel which it had converted into a clubhouse, with a clubmaster's house incorporated, at no little expense, the Society decided to advertise it, and in the next year the Society turned down a challenge from the Royal Musselburgh as a matter of principle which restricted matches with other clubs to Burgess alone, there having been voices raised at Council meetings which deplored such meetings with other clubs. Idle speculation is profitless of course, if unsupported by facts, but it seems that for a time at Musselburgh the Society was not the old open and harmonious community of spirits that it had so conspicuously been when domiciled at Bruntsfield, not even with the continuing presence of the stalwarts who did so much for East Lothian golf and Bruntsfield's reputation.

Nor in the end was the preference for Burgess a happy one. Bruntsfield stipulated that the Trophy which had hitherto been played for annually by the two clubs, should be a final match for permanent possession by the winner, whereupon Burgess declined, on the grounds that the conditions proposed by Bruntsfield departed from the original. Bruntsfield thereupon let the matter lapse, leaving the Trophy with Burgess, the current holders.

In the absence of reliable contemporary documentary evidence of the reasons why the original conditions of a popular fixture should be thus modified by a unilateral declaration, and the Burgess *Chronicle* states the facts accordingly, one must affect reticence and regretfully add that the rejection of the Royal Musselburgh challenge might have been even more unfortunate, for the Royal Musselburgh was an old and historic club too (1774), whose new Clubhouse (1873) was eventually to be a near and friendly neighbour, and whose Officer in 1810 had been instructed to intimate to the 'Fish Ladies' the prizes of a new creel and shawl and two of the best Barcelona silk handkerchiefs to the best female golfer who plays on the annual occasion on the 1st January next, a revealing and winsome promise likely to appeal to old Bruntsfield hands.

On 27 May 1886 the Society's new Musselburgh Clubhouse, by Hippolyte Blanc (architect of the Castle Great Hall, Portcullis Gate, St Margaret's Chapel, John Knox's House, St Cuthbert's Church West End, Mayfield Church, Christ Church Churchhill, etc. etc.), was opened for play. A grand dinner which echoed true Bruntsfield feelings with 'mirth and fun which made the echo to resound with jocund laughter', was quite in the old manner. And in a further return to the old manner a few weeks later Bruntsfield made amends with a resumption of the forsaken Burgess match. This happy event was due to the zeal and energy of the redoubtable Captain Bloxsam and the faculty he possessed of imbuing members with his own enthusiasm, as both *The Scotsman* and *The Field* testify in two exceedingly well-written accounts of the match and the psychological significance of the building of a new clubhouse which had revitalized a moribund Bruntsfield. The match was played at North Berwick, nineteen-a-side, and, by everyone except Bloxsam, Burgess was confidently expected to win hands down, but the decided thrashing which Bruntsfield was expected to suffer was not to be, and Bruntsfield won by nineteen holes, 55 to 36.

Thereafter the Society progressed peacefully and domestically and was principally concerned with the arrangement of fixtures, competitions, prize balls, and the admission of new members. In April 1888 a general meeting was held and attended by 38, which was considered to be the largest attendance for a long time, symptomatic of future prosperity. But the prosperity of the future was threatened by present deterioration of the green. In 1890 there was growing dissatisfaction with its condition despite the united efforts of the four private clubs which used it with proprietorial interest until 1894 when the links came under the administration of the Town Council. The Honourable Company's notable concern in the management of the green produced a series of annual 'Statements of Expenses' which disclose fascinating details of the practicalities of green-keeping of the time, and punctilious records of the memberships of the contributory clubs. Several of these statements have been found in the Society's papers.

They account for the years 1887, 1888, 1890, and 1893. The contributory clubs, the Honourable Company, Bruntsfield, Burgess, and the Royal Musselburgh, shared the expense of the upkeep of the green and were assessed according to their numbers. With 400 the Honourable Company regularly heads the lists, even for 1893 when its listed playing membership drops to 200, the Honourable Company having by that time left for Muirfield, in 1891. It retained an interest in its successor at Musselburgh however, and for an annual subsidy its members who had resisted the move to Muirfield continued to have the use of a hundred boxes and privileges of membership in the 'New Club'; rather like the Bruntsfield arrangement with the faithful remnant at Bruntsfield Links who were known as 'The Club'.

Bruntsfield is generally second in the lists with 130 or thereabouts, and Burgess fluctuated similarly with somewhat lesser figures around 100, the Royal Musselburgh entries wavering from 90 to 136. These clubs contributed

4/- per head yearly, except the Royal Musselburgh at 2/6, the difference being paid by the Honourable Company to make an equitable average annual due of 4/10 per member all round. The green-keeping details of the expenses incurred by the Hon. Co. include wages, hire of horse for roller, large and small roller, leather horse boots, grass cutters and hole cutters, flag shafts and wool for flags, painting flag rods, and carting road mud to the Links to fill up holes.

The principal competitions of the Society, the Gold Medal, the Cairns Medal, the Ladies' Cup and the Turnbull-Morrison Cup, continued to be played for, and on one occasion, in May 1892, the Gold, the Ladies' and the Turnbull were all won by a Mr J. Turner who had already won the Turnbull-Morrison twice. It thus became his property and vanished from the records. But despite the continuing activity, and the orthodox duties and management of a golf club satisfactorily accomplished within the Clubhouse, there was growing dissatisfaction with the green itself, which the departure of the Honourable Company and its initiative did nothing to improve. And there was more. The Musselburgh links were increasingly congested. The long oval had been enclosed for racing since 1816 and had an earlier grand-stand, but the grandstand of today was a work of 1886, the very year in which Bruntsfield's fine new clubhouse was opened, just a few yards away. What would the members think of that?

The clubhouses of the Honourable Company, Royal Musselburgh and Burgess were, in that order of appearance, further up the road and less intimately affected, but none was at all distanced from the commotions of Musselburgh Race Day (Plate 13). The army of two hundred white-coated bookmakers, high upon their stands in frenzied gesticulation to one another and the surging crowd about them, to tempt investors and layers of odds, the contingents of Fisherrow 'Fish Ladies' who numbered golfers among them, as we have observed, in striped petticoats, blue stockings, shawls, and Barcelona silk handkerchiefs, the oyster-sellers, whose wild and beautiful call of 'caller ou'' [fresh oysters] rang down the streets and squares of the New Town, the monkey grinders, ice-cream vendors, merry-go-rounds, travelling theatres and fortune-tellers, acrobats, jugglers and pickpockets, all provided something to write to the Secretary about.

There was much talk at the time of seeking a private green, away from public circumstances, and there was urgent discussion of the old situation. And there was considerable effort, shared by Burgess as well, to find suitable ground with golfing and clubbable possibilities, which the Honourable Company had already acquired at Muirfield further down the coast, further yet from Edinburgh. Burgess searched far and wide, considering Baberton, Ravelston, Duddingston, Blackford Hill, and Corstorphine, all nearer Edinburgh. Bruntsfield was similarly inclined, but did not repeat its abortive invasion of Holyrood Park, royal since the twelfth century no less, whereat with genuine but misguided official permission, when considering the move from Bruntsfield Links in years gone by, members had actually laid out a provisional course, by Peter McEwan, in the valley not far from Samson's Ribs. They were arrested in this amazing act and eventually appeared before the Sheriff and warned not to do it again.

In the restive circumstances of 1892 another suggestion was made, also vibrant with future possibilities. It came from an 'influential' member of Burgess, to propose an amalgamation of the two Societies, the disposal of one clubhouse and the sharing of the other. The suggestion reached the minute books of Bruntsfield but was not taken up, being strictly unofficial, as were Bruntsfield's inquiries about Archerfield, which got a dusty answer.

In a sense it was the Bruntsfield Links situation all over again: the need to go, the desire to stay, and an insistence in keeping what they had, whatever else. But new and powerful influences stimulated change, an accelerating improvement in the design and construction of clubs and balls, and a consequent need of new and different golf courses. And there was the railway line, reaching to Cramond Brig Station (Barnton) via Barnton Gate (Davidsons Mains), whose first preliminary sod was cut in October 1891.

CHAPTER 3

The Return to Edinburgh

The golfing aboriginals of Wright's Houses returned to Edinburgh about the same time. Burgess came first and opened its Barnton course in 1895, its Clubhouse in 1897. Bruntsfield's last formal play at Musselburgh was the Autumn Meeting for the Cairns and Hay Medals on 26 October 1897. Its migration followed in similar ways, course first, Clubhouse afterwards, on land in the Barnton estate.

The Burgess *Chronicle* records that Burgess initiated negotiations in October 1894, and 'forthwith obtained the first call on all the ground on the Barnton estate' (and it confesses doubt about whether or not they chose the best location). Be that as it may, Bruntsfield made an exploratory visit to the estate before the Autumn meeting at Musselburgh, doubtless encouraged by Burgess' success and the help which they could give them.

Among the hundreds of miscellaneous papers recovered from the deed boxes, from which much of the Society's early history has been deduced, there is one of fundamental significance in the Society's later history, which by great good fortune survives. It is an authentic record, written as a memorandum of what must have been the Society's first tentative approach to the landowner of the great Barnton/Cramond Regis estate.

The memorandum here considered consists of three pages of discoloured 'flimsy', very worn at the edges, in faded, longhand, with some uncertain words, duly noted. It is an account of a formal interview, probably written by a clerk at the dictation of the Society's solicitor, James Gibson, SSC, who was there. Because of its historical importance it is here quoted in full.

Memorandum of Interview between Messrs John Clark Brodie & Sons WS and James Gibson SSC 10 October 1897.

Mr Gibson saw Mr Mounsay [?] WS, one of the above firm, being the Partner who has charge of the Barnton estate. Mr Gibson without disclosing for whom he inquired was informed that while Sir James Maitland had not at one time seemed desirous of feuing the ground in question to the north of the Barnton Course, in respect [sic] he thought it might become more valuable for residential feus, yet, now, while he might not feu this he might entertain a proposal to lease. For definate [sic] reply, however, as to whether he would feu or lease the ground for a golf course application should be made direct to Sir James Maitland Bart. Private Secretary's Office, Stirling, and it might be suggested that a personal interview should be granted. Assuming he were willing to feu or lease there seemed no reason why the whole vacant ground to the north of the avenue should not be taken in, so far as required for 18 holes.

The Barnton Club had about 90 acres at £7–10/- an acre per annum. The ground was feued to them only to be used as a golf course or open space—not to be built on. They had no right to buy the ground. At fixed periods they could give up their feu. The clubhouse is held [?] on a separate feu.

If Sir James would not feu but was willing to lease then the lease would probably be for 20 or 30 years, and breaks might be stipulated for. The Clubhouse might be built on a piece of ground to be feued for the purpose and on such a plan as would enable it to be [feued] for villas or residences in the event of its ceasing to be used as a clubhouse.

In the event of a lease being granted it might be assumed that a less rent would be charged than the sum which would be [three words illegible] annual feu. The impression conveyed by Mr Mounsay [?] was that a proposal to lease would be entertained, but he did not seem to convey much hope of a feu being granted. He indicated that the ground was considered to be more valuable for residential feus than the Barnton Course.

A roadway was in course of formation which would make the site of the proposed Club about 3 minutes walk from Barnton Gate Station.

He seemed to indicate that the ground immediately to the south of the Barnton Railway running along the line between Barnton Gate Station and Cramond Brig Station would probably be more readily leased or feued by Sir James than the ground to the north of the Railway.

The advent of the railway pushing westwards from the city doubtless played its part in the search for a new home. On the single-line track from Princes Street Station to its terminus at Cramond Brig Station, where Burgess built its Clubhouse, with an audible bell to warn its members of train times, Barnton Gate Station ('Next stop Cramond Brig!') would serve Bruntsfield golfers very well, were they to succeed in acquiring the land they play over today.

They did. Following the exploratory visit which produced a hopeful plan of a future course and a memorandum of a conversation with the agents of Sir James Gibson Maitland the landowner, equally hopeful, the Society entered into negotiations with him and all went well. Which was just as well, for four preponderant questions had more or less simultaneously to be considered: the departure from Musselburgh and the consequent disposal or continued use of the Clubhouse there; the finding and acquisition of suitable land for a golf course and Clubhouse in or near Edinburgh; the erection of a new Clubhouse on that land; a fundamental change in the Society's status by incorporation under the Companies Act of 1862–69, to formalise its status, facilitate its conduct of affairs, and limit its liabilities, corporate and personal.

Accordingly, the Musselburgh Clubhouse and all that it contained came under the umbrella of a 'Musselburgh Clubhouse Company'. This especially created body bought the Clubhouse from the Society in May 1896, for £800, in order to lease it back to the Society for an annual rent of £70. Why? Why did the Society not cut the painter and sell outright to any buyer an extremely fine building scarcely ten years old and certain to command a good price?

Evidence is wanting which could answer this obvious question, for the minute book of the time records only the facts, not the reasons for them, but a likely hypothesis is that the contemplated departure from Musselburgh was thought to be a hazardous venture, especially at a time when the Society's financial state was causing concern, if we may judge from its conceding the use of the Clubhouse to lady golfers in their families at this very time, May 1896. The Directors were being prudent: should the hazardous undertaking fail the Society would still have the Musselburgh Clubhouse, in a sort of fall-back situation.

But in the changed and more hopeful circumstances which were to follow, the lease was renounced as from Whitsunday 1898, and desirable articles, furniture, etc., were eventually removed for use in the new Clubhouse at Barnton, Edinburgh. In April members were warned of the forthcoming termination of the lease and advised to remove personal belongings by the 14 May.

In their assiduous efforts to acquire new land the Directors steadily pursued the matter with Sir James. Quick and detailed agreement had been reached in November 1897, when he died, on the eve of a concluding meeting. Negotiations were not upset however. His daughter, later to be Patroness of the Society, generously declared herself 'to be wishful to carry out her late father's ideas', and thanked the Society for its kind expression of concern for her loss. In the fulness of time, as Patroness she formally declared the new Clubhouse open, on the 17 October 1899, exactly two years after the departure from Musselburgh.

The New Clubhouse and Course

The opening ceremony was a grand affair, and expected to be so. The Burgess, Royal Musselburgh, the New Club Musselburgh (successor to the Honourable Company there), Mortonhall, Duddingston, and the Corporation Golf Club were all invited to attend. Otherwise, invited guests were perforce limited to one per member. Captain Inches presented Miss Maitland with a gold key, and upon the door being opened the assembled gathering collected in the Dining Room, where she formally presented the 'Maitland Bowl' to the Society, in commemoration of the occasion. After tea a special train ('stopping at all stations'), which had left Princes Street Station at 2.37 for Barnton Gate returned therefrom at 4.45. The Directors hoped that the Society's uniform would be worn.

Exchanges with the Maitland interest were always courteous and understanding, for the gaining or losing of land, the adjustment of boundaries and the like, and during the Kaiser's war some twenty years later, when the Society was in financial difficulty and unsuccessfully trying to get a reduction of feu duty, the relationship was cordial still.

But we digress. In April 1898 plans for the Clubhouse were submitted to the Directors for approval, and through them to Miss Maitland, and thereafter to a Clubhouse Building Committee for further discussion with the architect, William B. Taylor, a member, and eventual possessor of an impressive golfing record forby, Cairns Medallist in 1894, 1897, 1898, 1900, 1903, and Gold Medallist in 1900. He won the Irish Amateur in 1895, 1896 and 1898, and was a distinguished member of a distinguished club, Mortonhall, as well.

The course meanwhile, which the proposed Clubhouse was to serve, was then in play in a tentative and experimental way. It was served by a Clubhouse whose foundations lie beneath a recent extension of the Clubhouse which Miss Maitland opened in 1899. Strictly speaking the course played today is approximately a year older than the Clubhouse of today and each has a separate feu charter, although each is an essential part of the original conception.

The hiatus between the playing on the one and the building of the other, and the fact that course and Clubhouse are the subjects of different feus, are advanced as likely explanations of the frequently expressed belief that the Clubhouse of today was originally erected with an alternative private residence in mind, in case the new and hazardous enterprise at Barnton might fail. The title deeds for the Clubhouse yield ambiguous evidence of the private house alternative, which it is imperative to examine. The preamble to the feu contract for example, dated as between the 21 and 28 September 1898, says '. . . the Feu shall be used by the vassals and their foresaids only as a site for a Clubhouse or a Dwellinghouse with suitable offices . . .'. This seems to be evidence enough, and it is reinforced by a 'Back letter' from Miss Maitland to the Society, 1898, referring to a 'Golf House or dwelling house'. But more legal papers of the same period, a Deed of Restriction included, refer to 'Golf Course and Clubhouse' only. A private house as a 'fall back' expedient is doubtful although consistent with the Directors' prudence regarding the Musselburgh Clubhouse.

One must approach the question with all due caution. It is inherently unlikely that the brief for the architect would embrace such an uncertain possibility, and he was specifically required to prepare a scheme for the accommodation of 500 members, not to cost more than £2000. Nor does a study of Taylor's later plans, sections and elevations (the originals are lost), support it, and all discussion of his accepted scheme, when doubts and alternatives would have been voiced and recorded, was about Clubhouse matters only. It is pardonable to suggest that the few and incidental references to a 'dwelling-house' refer to the possibility of residential staff accommodation within the Clubhouse building. It is so provided today. A later plan does indeed include this with three beds, bathroom, and sitting-room, for a Cook.

The inclusion of the words 'dwelling-house' in the feu charter, for one acre, would permit the erection of one to be seriously considered, should the need arise, but it never did. The hazardous enterprise was not a failure but a great success.

The hiatus between play and building was surely an inevitable consequence of progression in new territory, play first, with a temporary Clubhouse, a permanent Clubhouse afterwards. Burgess provides a similar history of development, as does Sunningdale, another Park creation.

The move from the links of Bruntsfield to those of Musselburgh was after all a move from one short and historic green to another equally short and historic. And both were on common land. After the migration to an extensive and historical estate there was to be a great difference in playing, and in the life of the Society. To raise money for the 'acquisition of a tract of ground at Barnton suitable for a private course' as many new members as were necessary for the purpose were admitted by dispensation of the Regulations hitherto more strictly observed, to bring the numbers up to 240. An unduly conservative estimate it turned out to be, for admissions rose steadily. At the end of 1899 a halt was called at 500. Numbers now played a part in membership considerations, and that part was financial, not social, nor gregarious, nor songster. The likeable and affectionate *Reminiscences* were not to be repeated, although Aitchison was still to the fore.

In every aspect of the Society's life, on and off the green, a feeling of fresh start is manifest, as though the move from Musselburgh and particularly from Bruntsfield was a wandering in the wilderness. Indeed, there had been not a few Bruntsfield members who showed no great excitement for the moves therefrom and said, as Mr Serjeant Buz Fuz would have said, 'the subject presents but few attractions'. In 1897 Bruntsfield and Burgess were in fact demonstrating a salmon-like instinct to return to the place of their breeding. Which is not precisely true maybe, but there are different kinds of truth, and the analogy is true enough, wholly authentic in spirit if only half-true in fact.

For Bruntsfield the flight from Musselburgh was not to acquire an existing course and play on common land, but to an entirely new one in a parkland estate. The Burgess course, which it immediately adjoins, was less trouble-some in the making, for it incorporated an earlier private course made by Robert Clark, author of the classic *Golf: a Royal and Ancient Game*, to which this history owes much. Himself a fine golfer and originator of the 'best ball' game, he was the first captain of the élite Roundell Club at Gullane, which of course included Bloxsam of Bruntsfield. Clark was a Bruntsfield man, and a Gentleman Golfer, instigator of the Honourable Company's departure from Musselburgh to Muirfield in 1891. With John Dunn he represented Bruntsfield in the famous inter-club tournament at St Andrews in 1857/8, whereof Bruntsfield's Robert Chambers, Amateur Champion-to-be in the following year, also participated, but for Musselburgh, representatives being limited to one foursome's pair per club.

Clark was a distinguished R & A medallist moreover, more than once, but alas, in its obituary notice *The Scotsman* relates a terrible experience which befell him at Musselburgh, 'shameful to tell though it seemed no shame to him to do', as the Anglo-Saxon chronicler wrote about William the Conqueror and his 'Domesday' Survey or income tax probe of 1085, *The Scotsman* reports that Clark was all square at the eighteenth. With one to play and all square he holed in one, and lost the match because he conceded, never thinking his ball would be in the hole. As Clark himself would have said, it was enough to make the angels weep (or at least some of them, for they cannot all be golfers).

He died in 1894, at Pau, the home of 'La Golf Club de Pau', the oldest golf club in Continental Europe. It was started in 1814 by officers of the Scots Guards (who else!), on leave from Wellington's regiments after the battle of Orthez in the Peninsular Wars. This remarkable early insertion of golf into a country hitherto innocent was formalized by the Duke of Hamilton and Brandon who consolidated and 'founded' this little bit of Scotland in the foothills of the Pyrenees, in 1856. What a story!

When the Directors decided to recruit an eminent pioneer of golf course architecture for development of land available on the estate of Sir James Gibson Maitland they made heartening declarations of intent: there were to be no delays, the layout of the course was to be agreed upon, and acted upon, forthwith. This was done.

It is of interest to know that in fact comparatively little had to be done, and to reflect that Scottish courses are made by Nature in one way and another and not by developers and earth-moving machinery, 'Make a green here, another there, keep that avenue of trees, use the carriage wash-pond as a hazard (at the present 5th'), among the unrecorded thoughts of the members who briefed Willie Park with helpful suggestions. It must have been a heartening experience for the pioneering members who were privileged to survey the parkland scene from the higher ground around the present 10th tee to visualise and to conjecture thus, conscious that their experience was one not to be repeated, that they were envisaging and creating a unique, true and permanent Bruntsfield course, at last. They did it well.

Willie Park

Burgess recruited Tom Morris and later James Braid for the original layout and subsequent modification of their Barnton course, and what could be better than that? But Bruntsfield commissioned the founder of golf course architecture, Willie Park, jnr., a Musselburgh man, author of the first book by a professional, *The Game of Golf*, which was appearing in the bookshops just when the Society was about to depart from Musselburgh and begin a new life. That was not bad either.

Willie Park, jnr., was twice Champion, in 1887 and 1889. He was renowned ballmaker and an inventive and accomplished clubmaker as well, and advertised his chief claim to early fame accordingly, 'Grounds surveyed and Reports made. Courses laid out and made by contract'. He ventured to America and the Continent and laid out courses in Britain besides, and was years before his time with an (unsuccessful) enterprise of combining a golf course with a housing development. And he wrote the stupendous words, 'a man who can putt is a match for anyone'. (Taylor retorted that a man who can approach has no need to putt.) Bruntsfield may justly be proud of its association with Willie Park. 'He belonged to the professional aristocracy of golf, the embodiment of all that is thorough and upright.'

At the time of leaving Musselburgh and making a new course there were significant changes in the game and its accessories which must grievously have affected the Bruntsfield golfers who were without a home and had to make one. It would of course be in the highest degree misleading to attribute changes in the social and golfing life of the Bruntsfield golfers only to the dramatic development in the design and construction of clubs and balls. Most golfers tend to take improvements and benefactions in a spirit of philosophic doubt, and continue their hopeful best regardless. But perhaps a few more general observations might here be included to help set the scene as it were.

For a few years before 1900, but taking that as a central date, we may identify a period of change and development in the game which particularly affected the laying-out of a new course and the modification of an old one. Strokes and distances, hazards, greens, fairways and rough, were all sensitive as never before to the improvements in material, design and construction, and consequently the capabilities, of club and ball, and it behoves us to remember in the by-going that as the game developed accordingly in wider horizons so did rules and regulations. The size of the ball for instance was for long quite unlimited. You could have any size you liked. It was not until after the First World War that the ball was sized and specified. The 'feathery' was described by weight, the most popular size being 26–28 dram, but in the Honourable Company's collection at Muirfield there is a monster of 33 drams. Persimmon for clubheads came in just when Bruntsfield members were trying to come to terms with their new green and the Green Committee, and later golfers will understand and sympathise with them as with grief and pain they toiled in the 'bunkers of repentance'.

There were members who came from Musselburgh who had gone there from Bruntsfield Links. They knew what a 'feathery' was, and for long had played with the 'gutty' which succeeded it in 1848 and was at its peak in 1890, but soon after they arrived at the great new parkland course at Barnton Gate and were settling in, the 'Haskell' arrived too. This was unsettling to be sure, a rubber-cored ball 'which did more to stimulate the game than any other development before or since', say Henderson and Stirk in their *Golf in the Making*. The tragedy of losing such a wondrous help to better golf can well be imagined, and with long grass and unresponsive sheep there were many dramas. But a concurrent development in the design and construction of clubs altered the very style of play as well.

James Braid, born in Elie, one of the Great Triumvirate, in ten years (1901–10) five times winner of the Open and three times runner-up, who 'lashed into the ball in a kind of divine fury' and belied a kind and thoughtful expression thereby, ('nobody could be as wise as James Braid looks'), could not have played like that with the traditional, elegant, long-headed woods. They would not have long survived the shock.

By 1890 they were fast becoming obsolete, except the putter, but many must have been brought to Barnton Gate for play on the new green. Herein resided a problem for the many members who came from Bruntsfield Links by way of Musselburgh and included in their armament the rubber-cored wound ball and the traditional slender long-headed club to hit it with, a 'villainous misuse' of a beautiful club-head made to sweep away a feathery or a gutty. The rubber-cored wound ball being more resilient and sitting up better than the gutty stimulated the style of the hitting blow by the 'bulger' driver with a short rounded head which Willie Park, jnr., claimed to have invented in 1884. Henry Lamb, an amateur from Angus, conspicuous at Sandwich, Kent, also laid claim to the invention, greatly to Park's annoyance, but a dubious distinction it was held to be by none other than Horace Hutchinson in 1890. He wrote of the inventor of the 'bulger' that his name 'stinks in the nostrils of all who see a thing of beauty in the delicate curves of a real thoroughbred head'. Nonetheless, the 'bulger' anticipated the wood of the future.

The styles of past and future are exemplified in the swing. In the old style the player stands back from the ball because he handles a long shaft with an elongated head and a flat lie. The shaft has much flexibility or whip. The modern player stands closer to the ball and wields a shorter and stiffer club with a rounded compact head. He does not sweep the ball away but delivers it a blow. He hits it. In witness and token of the old style we refer to two renowned portraits.

In 1771 Sir George Chalmers painted a famous portrait of William St Clair of Roslin, 'of noble eye and chastened pride', as Walter Scott said of him, who was Captain of the Honourable Company of Edinburgh Golfers in 1761, 1766, 1770 and 1771. The painting hangs in Archers' Hall in Edinburgh, the home of the Royal Company of Archers, the Queen's Bodyguard for Scotland, and rightly so, for bowmakers were clubmakers when 'woods' prevailed and 'irons' were exceptional. Not only that, the Archers compete yearly at Musselburgh Links where the Bruntsfield golfers once toiled, for the renowned Musselburgh Arrow, probably the world's oldest sporting trophy, played for in 1603 and maybe earlier than that, whose winner received 'a riddle of claret' from the Honest Toun.

The fascination of the portrait is the stance of St Clair. He is shown close-wigged and resplendent in full golf attire, flat Scottish bonnet, long scarlet coat, black breeches, white hose and buckled shoes. He stands away from the ball and holds a long-shafted club in widely-spaced hands. The club has an elongated head and a flat lie. But more important in the present dissertation is the fact that his front leg is well forward—the closed stance for the sweeping stroke of the early wood, misunderstood as being impossibly awkward, perhaps the artist's misdrawing? Not so.

We have also the famous portrait of Alexander McKellar, (Plate 16), the 'Cock o' the Green', who haunted Bruntsfield Links with obsessive enthusiasm and played all day and everyday and most of the night. He died *c*. 1813 and achieved immortality in Kay's *Portraits* which was published in 1838. Kay was an Edinburgh surgeon-barber with a gift for caricature of the highest order and his drawings and etchings constitute a valuable commentary on Edinburgh society of the time. Anybody who was anybody is in that book of nine hundred caricatures, including McKellar, who was drawn on the spot by the artist in 1803 during a special visit to Bruntsfield Links to do just that. The resemblance of the two portraits is altogether striking—same club, same set-up, left leg forward; the closed stance for the long sweeping action.

This was not the style of the Bruntsfield and Burgess golfers any more however, although hitherto they had played on historical 'greens' which had known it. On the contrary they had chosen to play golf where no golf had been played before.

It would be pardonable to assume that the immigrants to the Barnton estate simply resumed their interrupted play and carried on as usual, more or less, when they returned to Edinburgh. It was by no means as simple as that. There was nothing of a golf course to come to, nor a clubhouse, nor anything that could be one. Burgess to westward was more fortunate in this critical transition period, with temporary residence in the second Barnton House (the first was at Davidson's Mains), but no such luck favoured Bruntsfield.

Accordingly all haste was made to bring the new ground into play with a temporary clubhouse to serve it, even a ready-made one. An 'iron' building (presumably corrugated-iron), was noted to have been used as such at Dalry and an effort was made to purchase it and transport it therefrom for re-erection at Barnton. But the 'iron' building turned out to have a longer life where it was, and the idea was abandoned in favour of one which proposed the erection of a temporary wooden clubhouse. This was done in 1898. The wooden clubhouse served the members very well until its relegation to caddy-shed and eventual box-room overflow from the new-built permanent clubhouse. After advertisement the wooden clubhouse was 'removed' in 1905/6 by the Highland Committee of the United Free Church of Scotland, which had made the only offer for it, £30. The Box-room of the new permanent clubhouse was then extended, the boxes having been reserved for this.

While committees simultaneously debated improvements in one clubhouse and adjustments to the architect's plans for another, the Green and Works Committee with Willie Park in attendance looked into the future and anticipated possibilities a month before the Society took formal possession of its new land on 15 March 1898. Specifications for tree-felling and removal, grass-cutting and sheep grazing were discussed, and even at this early period of hopeful development and future pleasure dire thoughts of bunkers and other iniquities were debated. In 1900 it was resolved to revise and complete the laying-out of the course, and a year later, 'because turf on inland parkland requires rest at this early date', it was resolved experimentally to reverse the course during winter, to restrict play in certain damaged areas, and repeat the treatment in a winter arrangement, which was done in 1902, 1903, and 1904.

In fact, the return to Edinburgh engendered a lengthy period of moderate land management. It also inaugurated a new era in the Society's long history. 'The Annual Report of the Directors', still the definitive official statement of the Society's present condition and future prospects, was first issued in 1898, and was called 'the First Annual Report since incorporation'. Henceforth the Society looked back to the date of its incorporation as though to a birthday. According to the terms of the Act with which it had voluntarily complied in 1898 the Society welcomed it 'as affording a convenient and prudent method of conducting the future affairs of the Society . . . not by way of Share Capital, but by way of guarantee, under which the liability of members in the event of liquidation would be limited to £2.25.'

At the time questions were raised about the use of 'Ltd.' in the Society's title, and Counsel gave a learned recommendation. But at no time, then, before, or since, has there been even a suggestion that the historic name might be changed, that 'Bruntsfield Links' should be dropped.

It would be well to observe what the pioneers had to do. The clubhouse, being where it is, inevitably started play westwards, into the teeth of the prevailing west wind, still a penitential beginning. There was no other way to go. A northerly and more congenial start, downhill and sheltered, which could now be possible, was then impossible, for the course stopped at the Quarry Wood, at the present 10th green, beyond which there was no progress.

The quarry, incidentally, yielded stone for Charlotte Square, begun by Robert Adam in 1791 as the last element of the first New Town. The tracks of the quarry railway to Cramond Road are clearly to be seen, between the 10th green and the road, where there is an identifiable entrance in the walling by the roadside.

From the termination of the fenced land at Quarry Wood, which came into the Society's possession in July 1923, the boundary of Bruntsfield went shortly uphill towards the present fairway of the 18th and then turned back towards the clubhouse in a short home hole. The areas of the present car-park, upper practice ground and the 16th and 17th fairways were quite outwith the original feu. Eventually, as more land was acquired, round the perimeter mostly, the course was adapted in such a way as to provide three large practice areas. Few clubs are so favourably endowed.

The 1st hole has always been where it is today, more or less, and it was towards it that a provisional fairway was early laid out for inspection and approval. It so happens that it heads straight towards the Burgess course, after which with felicitous consequence it turns northwards towards the Cargilfield corner. Thus do Bruntsfield and Burgess rub shoulders for a yard or two. This allowed them in 1985 to join together in the celebrations of the Burgess 250th anniversary with a remarkable match, 4-a-side each, (Captain, Vice-Captain, Club Champion, and Professional), in a 1-hole Cross Country Challenge Match played in period costume with period clubs which despatched non-period golf balls from the one clubhouse to the other. Bruntsfield won, with 19 strokes to 26 by Burgess, both results an eye-opener for the following spectators. And there was also a mammoth series of thoroughly modern 18-hole games, 200-a-side!, which Burgess won.

The route to the Cargilfield corner has always been the same. In early days however it encompassed four holes, not three. Holes round the circumference of the course have varied somewhat both in numbering and in situation because of the acquisition from time to time of marginal land, (e.g. Gamekeepers Road, and wood, 1907) to preserve amenity and permit enlargement of the course 'to make it a first-class scratch course' according to a vibrant initiative expressed with practical determination in 1908, when the first Professional was appointed. Such a brave ambition would never have been expressed in the days of Bruntsfield Links and Musselburgh, even though the latter had accommodated six 'Opens'.

What one might term interior development was from earliest times motivated by desires difficult to reconcile with the very nature of the ground, namely, to avoid or at least to minimize parallel fairways, up and down, side by side. The modifications and adjustments resulting from countless meetings and recorded recommendations are clear to see. Surface indications of abandoned tee platforms, bunkers, and even greens, are evident for the alert and vigilant, especially when guided by the sketch plans of Mr Peter Bryce which have been separately printed for the society, and favoured by light and shadow. But it cannot be denied that the archaeology of the course is sadly confused by the continual readjustment of those lesser and more recognisable features which could not but be affected by the untiring ingenuities of the Green Committee, ever lying in wait to undo what had been done and do something else instead. Archaeologically speaking the uppermost letter in a wastepaper basket has the latest date, the lowest has the earliest—until disturbed—and so it would be rash to allocate a particular feature to a particular layout. The interest resides in the indications of development and the suggestion of long continuity and earnest endeavour.

Throughout the first twenty years and more of course development, (saving the War years), the principal trophies continued to be played for—the Gold, Cairns and Hay Medals, the Ladies' Cup, the later Maitland Bowl commemorating the opening of the clubhouse, and the Inches Putter commemorating the opening of the course. There was worry and debate about other things too, such as wartime crops, and sheep.

In growing inland areas which depended upon sheep to keep the grass down, to a degree scarcely realisable by the younger golfer of today, grazing rents were constant items in a council's deliberations. For the Bruntsfield Directors they continued predominantly until the end of 1926, when an expert's report (Sir Robert Greig's), on the advantages and disadvantages of sheep, were carefully considered. But the council of the time was pondering the advantages of money as well. Sheep had been here before. No sheep meant a loss of grazing rent of some £200 p.a. and an increase in green maintenance costs of some £100 p.a., it was averred. On the other hand, a financial loss thus incurred could be offset or justified by greater cleanliness round the course and the removal of a main source of damage to trees, greens, and bunkers, where sheep bedded down for the night after their day's work was done. (A boy and a girl received 12/- a week, each, and pails, for collecting the droppings, worth 2/6 per cartload). And there would be a considerable saving in the provision and erecting of protective wire-netting, fencing, and the like, already a charge upon the Society's resources, against those habits which could in no wise be endured.

Hesitancy is apparent. In 1926 a second horse was purchased, for the reaper in the rough, but simultaneously a mechanical tractor is discussed, for the first time. This idea soon prevailed, and furthermore a tractor requires no garage while a work-horse requires a stable, at Davidsons Mains, at a cost.

The Navy and the Great War

Much which affected the Society and its ways is social history and society's concern, not Bruntsfield's alone. Service in the clubhouse and on the course was with difficulty maintained with reduced staff and standards. The posts of Head Greenkeeper and Clubmaster were increasingly important and trouble-some to fill and sustain. But the Society played its part in the way which golf clubs could, by relaxing its limiting rules, by participating in matches in aid of sundry Service matters, hosting competitions and the like in aid of worthy causes, and making available the course to the dispossessed, such as the South Queensferry golfers who were victims of naval and military encroachment. Edinburgh schools were welcomed, and the Navy, herewith singled out for honourable mention because the spirit of its appreciation was more than merely dutiful in declaring what Bruntsfield had meant to the Fleet. Instances of gratitude generously expressed are always worth repeating.

Even before hostilities, in May 1913, naval officers were absolved from the usual requirement of a permit because of their short stay. Two years later exactly Admiral Brook, on behalf of the officers of the Fleet who had enjoyed the courtesy of the course, intimated their wish to make a presentation to the Society. This was gratefully turned down as quite unnecessary, as the Society was only too pleased to extend the courtesy of the clubhouse and the course to the officers, but, it was suggested, a picture of one of the battle-cruisers would be appreciated, a matter for Admiral Beattie's Chief of Staff to consider. Thus it came about that in midsummer 1915 the Flag Captain HMS *King Edward VII* requested on behalf of the officers stationed in the Forth the acceptance by the Bruntsfield Links Golfing Society of a water-colour painting of HMS *Iron Duke* as a mark of their appreciation of the hospitality and kindness shown by members of the Society during the stay of the Fleet in Scottish waters.

A couple of months later the Fleet Paymaster called upon the Secretary to say that the officers of the Fleet were desirous of making a present to all the servants, in the clubhouse and on the green, to mark their appreciation of the willing help and attention shown them. And in December of that year the officers of the Grand Fleet at Rosyth sent a substantial cheque to the Society, 'as a Xmas Box for the servants in the Clubhouse and on the Green', for the help they had received.

In September 1917 the Society received grateful letters from the Navy which now desired to pay green fees hitherto suspended as wartime concessions to serving officers. The Naval Secretary to the Commander-in-Chief, Rosyth, wrote in the following terms, 'I am desired by Admiral Sir Frederick T. Hamilton, GCVO, KCB, Commander-in-Chief, Coast of Scotland, to convey to you the following message which he has received from the Captain of the Fleet on the Staff of the Commander-in-Chief, Grand Fleet, representing Officers of the Fleet:

'In view of the very generous manner in which the Fleet has been treated by the Bruntsfield Links Golf Club in that they have had the freedom of the Club for the past three years, the Officers of the Fleet feel that the time has arrived when they should help to support the club, and therefore would like to pay a suitable green fee . . .', and he added, in less formal terms, 'Perhaps you would also express to the Secretary our grateful thanks for all that has been done for us in the past.' And he added furthermore that Sir Frederick Hamilton and other naval officers serving at Rosyth and other naval establishments in the Forth desired to be cordially associated with the above, and wished to express 'a general appreciation felt by all officers who have enjoyed the privileges of the Society's Course so generously extended to them by the Committee.'

When a formal expression of thanks would have done, this was reward indeed, but it was not all. On 22 November 1919 the Grand Fleet Cup was presented to the Society by Admiral Sir Charles Madden on behalf of the Officers of the Grand Fleet, and in May of the following year the 'conditions' were decided by the Council of the Society. They are adhered to still, every year.

With the Navy in strength in the Forth estuary, wartime anxieties about bombardment from the sea were satisfied. Without naval presence riparian establishments like Bruntsfield, however unwarlike, would indeed have been vulnerable, well within range of even the secondary armament of hostile vessels. But suggestions of insurance against this threat were rightly rejected by the Council of the Society which not so long ago had rejected suggestions of insurance against raids by hostile Suffragettes. While insurance against bombardment and raids by Suffragettes was thought to be unnecessary, air raids were a different thing however, and the Council acted accordingly.

In the event nothing dramatic happened, much of the course was given over to food production of one kind and another, and sheep were moving hazards. But when they were banished the grass grew and more balls were lost and there were loud cries for their return. Sheep in fact were indispensable until the development and use of heavy grass-cutting machinery.

Long grass and sheep did not themselves alone occasion an emotional reaction to the loss of a golf ball, never a laughing matter. In 1900, soon after play began at Barnton Gate, a letter on the subject was addressed to the Secretary. It is in friendly and humorous style, philosophises about the inevitability of golf balls entering one's garden, and looks forward to the decisions of the Bruntsfield Directors being a perpetual source of irritation. This was from the receiving end. Not so light-hearted however is another, of 1910, which reports the loss of a ball by the writer who drove it into a householder's garden (presumably along the 1st fairway), and saw it under the oriel window, but there being nobody visible could not have it thrown back, after which, the writer and his partner, having done eleven holes, looked to see if it were still there, which it was not. Nor did it come to the clubhouse.

Only an old ball was there offered, not the Thornton 'Red Star'. Inquiries and correspondence multiplied, whereupon the luckless householder, he of the oriel window, was eventually moved to declare that the ball question was always a vexatious one, and that the arrangement for return of the same was inadequate, and that he wished it to be known that he will not hand over nor allow to be handed over any balls found in his garden, nor will he then return them to the Secretary. Any found will be put in a box and later given to the Secretary for disposal as he thinks fit.

It is too easy to satirise householders' annoyances of the early nineteen hundreds. They were surely the natural consequences of a golfing invasion of private parkland hitherto disturbed only by grazing sheep. But there are powerful and ancient precedents for golfers' concern for absent golf balls. The Register of the Privy Council of Scotland, 1629–30, records the complaint of William and Thomas Dicksoun 'makers of gowffe ballis in Leith', against the injurious actions of James Melville, quartermaster in the Earl of Morton's regiment, who sent 'lawlesse souldiers' who took many golf balls after uttering 'manie threatenings and execrable oathes'. Their Lordships found Melville and his servants guilty of stealing nineteen 'gowffe ballis' most unwarrantably, and fined him accordingly.

In 1914 the Spring and Summer meetings were held, but not the Autumn. In 1915 no competitions were held, nor matches with other clubs, and the lists of the Society's losses 'on active service' began, firstly with Argylls, Black Watch, Royal Scots, and Gordons, to continue in like manner in each 'Annual Report of the Directors' until that for the year 1918, after which the obituaries are succeeded by notices of all the annual meetings of spring, summer and autumn, as before.

The last wartime obituary, a brief one of four names only, includes Lieutenant Tom Stevenson, 9th Royal Scots, the 'Dandy Ninth'. He was killed in action in the last weeks of the war, in August 1918. His father, a member of the Society, was soon to found the Tom Stevenson Cup in his memory, for he had been a truly remarkable young golfer. (His sister Charlotte, when Mrs J.B. Watson, won the 'Scottish Ladies' in 1920, 1921, 1922 and 1929.) In 1911 he won the Cairns Medal and the Philp Spoon and in May, June, July and autumn of 1913 he won the Gold Medal, the Victoria Cup, the Inches Putter, the Challenge Flagon and the Army Cup—in view of those successes it seems necessary to add that the Society was still at full strength, his successes unqualified—but the War put a stop to all that.

The Trophies

Pensive thoughts of this kind, and the background history of the Grand Fleet Cup, bring to mind distant thoughts too often overlooked today: the Maitland Bowl to commemorate the clubhouse, the Inches Putter to commemorate the course, the Cairns Medal and the Ladies' Cup for Musselburgh, (the latter by no means easy to explain); the Victoria Cup to commemorate her reign, and the Gold Medal, the oldest of all, which had to be played for 'in the full uniform of the Society', commemorating nothing in particular save the supremacy of the holder and the legacy of Bruntsfield Links, where alone it was played for as early as 1819.

In the allegedly male-dominated society of the 1870s one may search in vain for the donors of the Ladies' Cup and ask who were the Ladies, and why? Was the Cup from them, or for them? A too-obvious explanation is that it was from the ladies of the golfers. This explanation has the merit of simplicity but lacks conviction. A clue is advanced in that statement, previously referred to, in the Society's minute book dated 22 May 1896, which concedes the use of the clubhouse to lady golfers in their families. This Musselburgh concession at least recognises their existence as golfers worthy of the first consideration and innocent of high crimes and misdemeanours, but it is sadly out-of-date in respect of the Ladies' Cup which is recorded as having first been played for in 1874, on Musselburgh Links, where the 'Fish Ladies' played a good game in 1810, and earlier it would seem, (p.33). The truth of its origins is not beyond serious doubt, and failing reliable verification we must admit defeat, but a later and reliable account invests its history with unusual interest. The trophy was lost, and found again, in an antique shop. Before it was found a replica had been made, and so the replica has never been used; but it occupies a historic niche in the Society's treasury.

The trophies have their own history; the winners' names come later. Not just casual donations to the prize list, although several were destined or designed to fill a gap in it, they signalise special people or commemorate special occasions, all worthy of remembrance from time to time.

A History such as this, economical in details of course development and clubhouse occurrences, would be unworthy without mention of its very fine War Memorials. They are in fact two in one, architectural, in wood, with names. As is frequently found elsewhere, the later is a postscript to the first, which was unveiled on 12 February 1921. It was designed as an overmantel for a new fireplace at the south end of the dining room, by Mr J. McLachan, an architect member. To it smaller panels in the same style and detailing were becomingly added by him in 1948. The composition agreeably closes the long vista of the dining room at one end; windows overlook the course at the other end, and along one side.

Although there had been 'an extensive scheme of alterations' in 1908/09, and adjustments continuously thereafter, the course was 'reconstructed' by golf course architect Dr A. Mackenzie to an extent sufficiently important to require an inauguration match in April 1922. While not so eventful perhaps as that of Luffness New which was won by the diminutive 'Leither', Ben Sayers, (the 'Wee Yin'), who was trained as an acrobat and turned cartwheels on the green at the drop of a ball, but important enough to occasion a foursomes celebration match with the Burgess golfers, who won. The 'reconstruction' gave the Society 'a Course which has been very greatly improved', when the Society's interests and active involvements were expanding in local and national golfing affairs, such as the formation of a Scottish Golf Union and the promotion of a Scottish Amateur Golf Championship, both initiated in 1920. Likewise the Society increased its play with other clubs, individually and in tournaments, in an accelerating post-war recovery.

A milestone in the Society's administrative progress was passed in October 1914 when the Directors bowed to the inevitable and decided to appoint, for the first time in the Society's existence, a permanent and fully salaried secretary, to administer the Society's ever-widening horizons, growing affairs and commitments, and to install him in an office in the clubhouse so that he could exercise daily more supervision than was thought possible by a part-time secretary, however assiduous and competent. This is the historic 'foundation-date' of the secretaryship.

But an understanding of the true nature of a society is not to be derived exclusively from its practical interests and achievements, however effective and beneficial. Its true nature resides in a historical continuity of thought and feeling, without which there is no 'History', only a 'Record'. Attention has been directed in the pages above to the Society's early spirit of friendly informality, and before the onward movement of 'history' becomes the static 'record' of happenings, it would be well perhaps to instance two examples of a generous concern for the well-being of its staff, 'in the Clubhouse and on the Green', as the Navy expressed it when acknowledging help and kindness received. Two examples will here suffice. They commemorate kindly thoughts no less than trophies do. The examples cited are years apart and demonstrate that continuity of thought and feeling which is still a lively characteristic of the Society and was early evident at Bruntsfield Links and Musselburgh.

Among the miscellaneous papers which the Society has inherited from its recent past is an old, small, notebook of the cheapest kind. It is stained with many beer or wineglass rings and it was 'Manufactured by T. Houlden, Stationer, 9 Nicholson Street, Edinburgh'. Otherwise it is a non-book, except that on the first of its few handwritten pages is the legend 'Inventory of Articles belonging to the Bruntsfield Links Golf Club; 1st January 1855.' It itemises the contents of the 'Dining Room', the 'Front Box Room', the 'Back Box Room', and the 'Kitchen', no more, and that of simple and frugal utility. It gives no indication of where this clubhouse was, except perhaps on the last page, which goes as follows: '1st January 1855. I hereby certify that the foregoing is a complete list of the Articles belonging to the Bruntsfield Links Golf Club, given in charge to Mrs Fraser, and a Copy of the same has been handed to her as authorised by Minute of Club Meeting dated 30th December 1854': (signed) John Forrest, Secretary, BLGC.'

As the long-serving Mrs Stewart was probably in action at Bruntsfield Links at this time, and as a Mrs Fraser was the wife of the Society's clubmaster at Musselburgh in 1876, when she died, it is possible that the Mrs Fraser of the Inventory of 1855 is the Mrs Fraser who died in 1876, and that the inventory refers to a Musselburgh clubhouse, of a sort, probably in Mill Hill. Be all that as it may, the recorded death of a clubmaster's wife instances the generosity of the Society at that time, for every sad detail of the unhappy event, shroud, coffin, hearse, and grave expenses, was met by the Society, probably in a time of need.

Likewise years later, at Barnton in 1916, the Society rallied round Head Greenkeeper Gault and his family, for he was 'most assiduous in his duties and to his exertions and care much of the present excellence of the Course was due'. He and his family suffered much bad health, but for long periods in the Infirmary he was kept at full pay, while employment on the course was found for his young sons. When he died at the age of forty-one, and left a family of eight, of whom the oldest was nineteen the youngest little more than a year, the Society, at the behest of members, raised a fund for their support, to be administered by the Directors.

The 1920s and Later

Between the Society's early life at the historic Links of Bruntsfield and of Musselburgh, and the return to Edinburgh about 140 years later, there is a great gulf fixed. We miss details of the early life; we would like to know more about that inventory of 1855, and about the problematical Mrs Fraser who was shown a copy of it. The accommodation inventoried therein is tantalisingly descriptive of chairs and tables and household goods, but impossible to locate. Because of such haphazard lack of detailed evidence the early history of the Society has here been painted with a broad brush, which on the whole is perhaps no bad thing for a narrative history of some 140 to 150 years, but after that, which brings the story to 1920 or thereabouts, when the Society and its course were settling down to a hopeful and permanent life together, generalised and developing history diminishes and a record of events succeeds it, which will be briefly stated.

It seems advisable to do so in categories of 'the course and its golfing occasions', and 'clubhouse affairs'. Taking the course and golfing occasions first in a selection from the official records, we cannot fail to note many 'reconstructions', even after the celebrated opening of the new course in 1922.

Improvements and modifications of no little importance have occurred since then, but notwithstanding such interruptions notable events have indeed occurred as well: His Royal Highness the Prince of Wales became an Honorary Member in 1924, the Scottish Professionals' Annual Meeting in 1926 was granted the courtesy of the course. Speedily thereafter followed the Society's resumption of fixtures with Officers of the Navy (Grand Fleet, 1927, Atlantic Fleet 1928, Home Fleet 1936); in 1933 Enid Wilson and Walter Hagen lost to Jack MacLean and W.B. Torrance. In 1937 the Boys' Amateur was granted the courtesy of the course and clubhouse, which occasioned Burgess to reciprocate in favour of the dispossessed. A course record of 70 was made by J.S. Graham in that year. It has since been broken, by A.G.G. Miller, with a 69, and broken again by A.W. Ritchie with a 64 in 1991.

In 1940, as part of the War effort, Henry Cotton and Dick Burton played an exhibition match in aid of the Red Cross Appeal Fund (the scores and balls used are mounted and on display in the Trophies Cabinet). Continuing War efforts put 26 acres of the course under plough by 1942, but the Boys' Championship lost no time after the War and resumed golfing hostilities in 1946, ploughing or no ploughing.

The Society's Professional J.S. Anderson won the 'East of Scotland' in his first Bruntsfield year, 1948, in which year Don Bradman and the Australian cricketers were welcomed and entertained by the Society. In 1955 Peter Thomson (70 and 65) played Antonio Cerda (72 and 70) in an exhibition match, and Anderson qualified for the St Andrews Open with a 74 and a 67, and thereafter had rounds of 71, 72, 77, and a 69, which was the best score of the final round. The service record of Professional Anderson, who retired in 1965 after 17 years, was beaten in 1966 by Head Greenkeeper Newlands with a record-breaking 52 years. These men were succeeded, respectively, by Burns and Harry Smith, both also of long service. The published Annual Report for 1961 records the 200th Anniversary Celebrations of the founding of the Society in 1761 (an arbitrary date it must be, for there is no discoverable evidence to sustain it. (See page 16). There was a grand dinner, with distinguished guests, and among nine invited clubs a tournament, won by the R & A team. In 1975 the British Boys' Open was played over the course; Marchbank beat Lyle, and both turned professional. Throughout the 1980s much concern and action were directed against elm disease, and this continues, with unprecedented determination and vigour in felling and replacement of affected trees.

'Family Tickets' were introduced in 1927 and '5-Day' memberships began in 1964 with a first intake of 23. In 1968 pictures by distinguished Scottish artists, Henderson Blyth, Houston, McTaggart and others, were purchased, and two stained glass panels were obtained from the Musselburgh Clubhouse (probably from Bruntsfield Links originally) and a trophy, 'The Bruntsfield Quaich', was presented to the Brunton Wire Mill Social Club, now owners and occupiers of the old Clubhouse, in grateful thanks for its care and generosity. The Captain's Medal of *c.* 1800, with its names of Captains since 1793, was stolen in 1968 and never recovered, but next year was replaced by a replica. In 1978 the clubhouse flat was extended, and the Secretary's office below it. The members' lounge of today, with its splendid panoramic wall, all glass, wrapped round a corner of the original Clubhouse of 1897, is the work of an architect member, the late J.A.H. Mottram.

The Society has in recent years become more expansive in its own affairs, and widening horizons have in different ways occasioned a junior membership in 1981, and in 1984 additional amenities in a lounge for visiting clubs and a mixed lounge for members and guests. A new locker room and ancillary buildings were opened in 1987.

APPENDIX 1

Trophies and Winners
by
M. W. Walton

CLUB CHAMPIONSHIP
CHIENE CUP

Presented to the Society in 1930 in memory of Professor John Chiene CBE who had been Captain from 1904 to 1905 and then an Honorary Member from 1913.
Awarded to the winner of the Club Championship.

1931	R.M. Carnegie	1961	A.R. McInroy
1932	G.T. Chiene	1962	C.N. Hastings
1933	H.R. Sturrock	1963	I.W. Hall
1934	J.S. Graham	1964	C.N. Hastings
1935	K.F. Gibb	1965	R.P. White
1936	V.E.D. Haggard	1966	R.P. White
1937	K.F. Gibb	1967	G.E. Robertson
1938	R.M. Carnegie	1968	R.P. White
1939	A.F. Simpson	1969	P.M.B. Bucher
1940		1970	P.M.B. Bucher
1941		1971	P.M.B. Bucher
1942		1972	P.M.B. Bucher
1943		1973	R.P. White
1944		1974	R. Reid Jack
1945		1975	A.F. Brown
1946	G.W. Mackie	1976	P.M.B. Bucher
1947	J.R. Ness	1977	A.F. Brown
1948	J.W.St.C. Scott	1978	A.D. Carnie
1949	A.M.M. Bucher	1979	A.F. Brown
1950	R.M. Lees	1980	P.M.B. Bucher
1951	A.F. Simpson	1981	M.G. James
1952	C.H. Johnston	1982	P.M.B. Bucher
1953	R.M. Lees	1983	P.M.B. Bucher
1954	J.M. Cowan	1984	D.M. Simpson
1955	C.M. Meek	1985	K.W. Aitken
1956	C.M. Meek	1986	A.F. Brown
1957	A.K. Shiel	1987	G. Duff
1958	J.W.St.C. Scott	1988	A.F. Brown
1959	R.M. Lees	1989	A.M. Anderson
1960	F.G. Dewar	1990	A.D. Carnie

HOLE AND HOLE COMPETITION
CHALLENGE SILVER FLAGON

Inaugurated by the Society in 1883 and awarded to the winner of the Hole and the Hole Competition.

Year	Winner	Year	Winner
1902	D.A. Callander	1935	K.F. Gibb
1903	R. Kay Jr.	1936	W. Wallace
1904	T.M. Ronaldson	1937	G.F. Hunter
1905	A.R. Simpson	1938	G.T. Chiene
1906	Wm. Macrae	1939	G.M. Fairbairn
1907	D. Currie	1940	
1908	R. Kay Jr.	1941	
1909	D.H. Dixson	1942	
1910	R. Davidson	1943	
1911	A.I. Banks	1944	
1912	R. Dixson	1945	
1913	T. Stevenson	1946	J.R. Ness
1914	H.L. Warden	1947	J.R. Ness
1915		1948	J.R. Ness
1916		1949	J.R. Ness
1917		1950	R.M. Lees
1918		1951	J.R. Ness
1919	A. Burn–Murdoch	1952	J. Malloch
1920	A.L. Robson	1953	C.N. Hastings
1921	A.L. Robson	1954	J.H. Ness
1922	A. Burn–Murdoch	1955	T.I.L. Burns
1923	J. Cairns	1956	R.H. Miller
1924	W.A. Ireland	1957	A. Hawley
1925	W. Macrae	1958	D.F. Macrae
1926	R. Scott	1959	J.A. Lang
1927	J. Field	1960	A.L. McClure
1928	R. Cairns Jr.	1961	G.G.I. Cameron
1929	R.M. Carnegie	1962	P.G.H. Younie
1930	K. Gibb	1963	C.N. Hastings
1931	T.R. Tod	1964	M.J. Sands
1932	D. Rodger	1965	C.N. Hastings
1933	R.M. Carnegie	1966	H.L. McKIll
1934	J.A. Shore	1967	W.B. Abbott

1968	H.H. Millar	1980	I.W. Hall
1969	I.W. Hall	1981	P.C. Millar
1970	W.M. Moncur	1982	J.M. Souness
1971	A.G. Donald	1983	D.M. Simpson
1972	W. Hutton	1984	L.I. Fletcher
1973	I.S. Morrison	1985	J.S. Hodge
1974	L.R. Tweedie	1986	R.G. Robertson
1975	R.M. Lees	1987	D.W. Ferguson
1976	I.W. Hall	1988	S.P. Riddell
1977	I.W. Hall	1989	I.W. Hall
1978	I.A.C. Whyte	1990	J.A. Crerar
1979	A. Bateman		

PHILP SPOON

Believed to have been presented to the Society by J.H. Inches when he was Captain.
Awarded to the runner-Up in the Hole and Hole Competition.

1900	J.H. Inches	1932	C.C. Robson
1901	J.H. Hood	1933	G. Romanes
1902	A.B. Alexander	1934	W.A. Ireland
1903	W. Adams Jnr.	1935	A.D. Crichton
1904		1936	E. McDiarmid
1905	D.N. Cotton	1937	J.C. Smith
1906	A. Banks	1938	W.R. Russell
1907	J.C.M. Bell	1939	G.W. Mackie
1908	A. Hood	1940	
1909	H.B. Dunlop	1941	
1910	R.A. Bruce	1942	
1911	T. Stevenson	1943	
1912	D.M. Wood	1944	
1913	A.I. Banks	1945	
1914	A. Burn-Murdoch	1946	
1915		1947	G.F. Poole
1916		1948	A.D. Mackenzie
1917		1949	I.A. Valentine
1918		1950	W. Carnie
1919	T.W. Dewar	1951	W. Carnie
1920	C.C. Robson	1952	J.M. Sturrock
1921	J. McLachlan	1953	N.A. Gray
1922	P. Galloway	1954	P.R. Bryce
1923	E.A. Burn-Callander	1955	W.G.F. Carnie
1924	C.T.F. Pearson	1956	C.M. Meek
1925	K. Henderson	1957	R.M. Lees
1926	J.F. Carnegie	1958	R.J. Normand
1927	R.H. Fraser	1959	J.H. Ness
1928	G.T. Chiene	1960	J.M. Sturrock
1929	G.W. Harper	1961	J.D. Cunningham
1930	R.H. Fraser	1962	P.L. Stewart
1931	H.H. Monteath	1963	L.C. Young

1964	G.K. Thomson	1978	I.D. Cochrane
1965	P.G.H. Younie	1979	D.M. Simpson
1966	D.F. MacRae	1980	D.R.M. Mitchell
1967	P.R. Bryce	1981	L.A. Thain
1968	J.G. Banks	1982	E.M. Donaldson
1969	R.M. Lees	1983	G.A. Duff
1970	R.M. Lees	1984	I.S. Morrison
1971	I.A.C. Whyte	1985	D.K. Anderson
1972	J.G. Banks	1986	J.R. Nicolson
1973	H.J.L. Allan	1987	D.M. Simpson
1974	G.S.P. Bain	1988	A.J. Deans
1975	I.A.C. Whyte	1989	G.C. Ellis
1976	M.R.S. Bateman	1990	C.N. Hastings
1977	A.J.R. Ferguson		

TOM STEVENSON CUP

Presented to the Society in 1920 by James St.C. Stevenson in memory of his son, Lieutenant Tom Stevenson, 9th Royal Scots, killed in action.

Tom Stevenson featured prominently in the Society's competitions during the period 1911 to 1914 by winning the Cairns Medal, Inches Putter (twice), Silver Flagon, Victoria Cup, Services Cup (twice), Philp Spoon and Gold Medal (twice).

It is awarded to the winner of the first competition of the Society's Golfing Season.

1920	R.A. Bruce	1945	
1921	J.S. Barker	1946	D.A. Sibbald
1922	F.B. Allan	1947	N.W. Graham
1923	J. Hodgson	1948	C.R.D. Leeds
1924	I.R. Macleod	1949	D.J. Colvin
1925	A.L. Robson	1950	W.C. Hopekirk
1926	J.F. Carnegie	1951	A.A. Lumley
1927	P. Donald	1952	C.N. Hastings
1928	J. Cairns	1953	C.M. Meek
1929	M.P. Galloway	1954	J. Malloch
1930	W.C.A. Ross	1955	G.I.L. Somerville
1931	H. Alexander	1956	R.G. Manson
1932	F.H. Hunter	1957	R.M. Lees
1933	G. Kay	1958	I.F.B. Stewart
1934	C.W.L. Miller	1959	M.H. Cullen
1935	R.M. Carnegie	1960	G.G.I. Cameron
1936	G.F. Hunter	1961	P.R. Bryce
1937	G.F. Hunter	1962	D. Sharp
1938	R.A.P.R. Kidston	1963	J.M. Sturrock
1939	D.G. Munro	1964	I.W. Hall
1940		1965	M.R. Green
1941		1966	A. Smart
1942		1967	C.H. Johnston
1943		1968	R.R. Orchard
1944		1969	E.K. Cameron

1970	H.N. Macphail	1982	N.R. Kay
1971	J.M. Gibson	1983	M.B. Auld
1972	R.A. Davie	1984	A.J. Loudon
1973	D.H.R. Ness	1985	A.S. Douglas
1974	T.A. Fairburn	1986	A.H. Johnstone
1975	D.N. Maxwell	1987	J.G. Buchanan
1976	D.W. Ferguson	1988	W.C. Skinner
1977	N. Fort	1989	T.A. Buttery
1978	H.H. Lumsden	1990	A. Skinner
1979	J.D. Crerar		
1980	I.E. Cochran		
1981	J.I. Wilson		

SPRING MEETING
GOLD MEDAL *The Society's Oldest Medal*

Presented in 1819 and sadly not engraved during 1846/48. It is awarded to the player returning the best Scratch Score in the Spring Meeting.

Notable winners include

S. Aitken 7 times between 1825 and 1842
R.T. Galloway 5 times between 1849 and 1854
R. Chambers 5 times between 1859 and 1868
D. Currie 8 times between 1901 and 1911

1819	J. Smith	1841	S. Aitken
1819	H. Graham	1842	S. Aitken
1820	J. Gray	1843	J. Stewart
1820	J. White	1844	A. Scott
1821	H. Graham	1845	A. Scott
1822	E. Henderson	1846	
1823	H. Graham	1847	
1824	A. McQueen	1848	
1825	S. Aitken	1849	R.T. Galloway
1826	W. Lothian	1850	R.T. Galloway
1827	A. Sanson	1851	R.T. Galloway
1828	S. Aitken	1852	W.H. Cameron
1829	W.M. Dymock	1853	R.T. Galloway
1830	J. Miller	1854	R.T. Galloway
1831	J. Stewart	1855	J. Sibbald
1832	J. Stewart	1856	J. Dunn
1833	J. Mitchel	1857	R. Clark
1834	S. Aitken	1858	A. Sheill
1835	A. Milne	1859	R. Chambers
1836	S. Aitken	1860	R. Clark
1837	J. Miller	1861	R. Chambers
1838	S. Aitken	1862	J. Bryson
1839	W. Dunbeech	1863	A. Fulton
1840	S. Aitken	1864	J. Bryson

1865	R. Chambers	1905	D. Currie
1866	A. Usher	1906	D. Currie
1867	J.K. Chalmers	1907	C.D.O. Morrison
1868	R. Chambers	1908	D. Currie
1869	W. Lees	1909	D. Currie
1870	J.T. Cunningham	1910	D. Currie
1871	J.T. Cunningham	1911	D. Currie
1872	J.T. Cunningham	1912	R. Kay Jr.
1873	W. Elder	1913	T. Stevenson
1874	W. Elder	1914	T. Stevenson
1875	W. Elder	1915	
1876	J. Whitecross	1916	
1877	A. Usher	1917	
1878	A.S. Douglas	1918	
1879	St.C. Cunningham	1919	A.M. Mackay
1880	A. Bryson	1920	A.R. Muirhead
1881	A. Bryson	1921	A.L. Robson
1882	A. Bryson	1922	A. Burn–Murdoch
1883	J.R. Whitecross	1923	A.L. Robson
1884	A.S. Douglas	1924	R. Cairns Jr.
1885	W.G. Bloxom	1925	A.L. Robson
1886	W.G. Bloxom	1926	A.R. Muirhead
1887	A.S. Douglas	1927	E.B. Dickson
1888	A.S. Douglas	1928	A. Burn–Murdoch
1889	J. Taylor	1929	R.N. Finlay
1890	D. Maclaren	1930	J.S. Graham
1891	J. Turner	1931	G.T. Chiene
1892	J. Turner	1932	G.T. Chiene
1893	T.T. Gray	1933	H.D. Fairbairn
1894	T.T. Gray	1934	J.A. Shore
1895	T.T. Gray	1935	G.T. Chiene
1896	C.S. Halkett	1936	J.A. Shore
1897	C.S. Halkett	1937	A.G. Thornton
1898	J. Taylor	1938	J.S. Graham
1899	C. Hay	1939	J.A. Shore
1900	W.B. Taylor	1940	
1901	D. Currie	1941	
1902	W.R. Taylor	1942	
1903	D. Currie	1943	
1904	M.M. Craig	1944	

1945		1968	A.K. Shiel
1946	G.G. Fowler	1969	P.M.B. Bucher
1947	G.W. Mackie	1970	R.A. Davie
1948	G.W. Mackie	1971	L.S. Hinchcliffe
1949	C. Hastings	1972	R.R. Jack
1950	P.R. Bryce	1973	R.A. Davie
1951	A.F. Simpson	1974	A.F. Brown
1952	R.M. Lees	1975	R.M. Rowberry
1953	J.H. Lamb	1976	P.G.H. Younie
1954	R.M. Lees	1977	L.S. Hinchcliffe
1955	G.W. Mackie	1978	R.H.J. Mackie
1956	T.C. Scott	1979	A.F. Brown
1957	J.H. Lamb	1980	A.F. Brown
1958	A.M.M. Bucher	1981	R.M. Rowberry
1959	R.M. Lees	1982	P.G.H. Younie
1960	T.C. Scott	1983	D.M. Simpson
1961	F.G. Dewar	1984	C.N. Hastings
1962	A.M.M. Bucher	1985	D.M. Simpson
1963	F.F. Kellow	1986	A.G.G. Miller
1964	R.H.J. Mackie	1987	D. May
1965	P.R. Bryce	1988	J.H. Bryce
1966	R.H.J. Mackie	1989	A.D. Carnie
1967	W.B.M. Laird	1990	G.A. Duff

SPRING MEETING
LADIES' CUP

Presented to the Society in 1873 and at some stage it was lost or stolen. A duplicate is in the display cabinet but was never used as the original was eventually recovered from a junk shop.

Awarded to the player returning the best net score in the spring meeting.

1874	W. Bryce	1904	C. Symington
1875	W. Croall	1905	D. Drummond
1876	C.N. Cowper	1906	A. Hutcheson
1877	M. MacGregor	1907	G.A. Fraser
1878	A.S. Douglas	1908	A.G. Thornton
1879	St.C. Cunningham	1909	F.G. Hart
1880	G. Ritchie	1910	T.W. Dewar
1881	G.F. Scott	1911	A.M. Bucher
1882	W. Kirkhope	1912	D. Fordyce
1883	A.M. Brown	1913	H.D. Thomas
1884	W. Reid	1914	L.S. Shennan
1885	J. Pringle	1915	
1886	G. Morrison	1916	
1887	J. McGlashan	1917	
1888	J. Turner	1918	
1889	W. Bryce	1919	D.A. Clapperton
1890	J.D. Paterson	1920	C.C. Robson
1891	J. Turner	1921	H.J. Jones
1892	J. Turner	1922	T.A. Wright
1893	J. Ainslie	1923	D.C. Steel
1894	W.F. Buist	1924	J. Aikman
1895	T.J. Gray	1925	J.A. Wright
1896	C.S. Halket	1926	H.J. Jones
1897	W. Andrew	1927	H.L.C. Guthrie
1898	J.M.S. Shaw	1928	H.L.C. Guthrie
1899	T.M. Ronaldson	1929	J.F. Reekie
1900	D. Currie	1930	F.W. Martin
1901	H. Rose	1931	G.A. Fraser
1902	H.D. Thomas	1932	W. Weeks
1903	W. Burt	1933	C.W.L. Millar

1934	S.C. Urquhart	1963	F.F. Kellow
1935	H.H. Monteath	1964	R.H.J. Mackie
1936	T. Park	1965	D. Sharp
1937	D.W. Gordon	1966	G.W. Mackie
1938	W.R. Russell	1967	A.C. Stepney
1939	J.L. Graham	1968	P.C. Millar
1940		1969	C.A. Carlow
1941		1970	A.P. Gray
1942		1971	H.N. Macphail
1943		1972	R.R. Jack
1944		1973	M.H. Cullen
1945		1974	A.F. Brown
1946	T.G. Duncanson	1975	G.A. Latta
1947	A. Dunbar	1976	J.A. Morton
1948	J.A. Jack	1977	A.H. James
1949	A.M. Grant	1978	I.D. Blackhall
1950	W.W. Mackay	1979	G.B. Ross
1951	W. Carnie	1980	S.D. Grant
1952	T.W.W. Davie	1981	S.H. Cruden
1953	J.H. Lamb	1982	B.A. Cadzow
1954	J.H. Ness	1983	J.D.L. Fairbairn
1955	T.I.L. Burns	1984	J. Nicolson
1956	T.C. Scott	1985	D.L. Millar
1957	J.H. Lamb	1986	G.C. Grieve
1958	I.F.B. Stewart	1987	W.W. Stewart
1959	R.M. Lees	1988	A.G. Young
1960	J.M. Burnet	1989	P.G. Renton
1961	J.A. Lang	1990	T.C. Bell
1962	A.M.M. Bucher		

C.E. SALVESEN TROPHY

Presented to the Society in 1957 by C.E. Salvesen to be played for by Members who admit to being 65 years of age or over.

1958	W.A. Davidson	1975	A.T. Boe
1959	W.A. Davidson	1976	A.F. Anderson
1960	K. Paterson Brown	1977	W. Clark
1961	J.L. Graham	1978	P. Whyte
1962	G.W. Brodie	1979	R.J. Normand
1963	J.S. Adam	1980	G.L.T. Henry
1964	J.A. Alexander	1981	P. Whyte
1965	J.A. Wright	1982	A.A. Hughes
1966	Sir S. Davidson	1983	V.F. Barnett
1967	A.M. Fraser	1984	J. Watson Forbes
1968	A.M. Fraser	1985	A.M. Lamont
1969	A.M. Fraser	1986	E.D.E. Dobbs
1970	W.F.G. Normand	1987	J.W. Elliot
1971	J.A. Wright	1988	J.W. Elliot
1972	D.G.L. Lackie	1989	D.A. Hill
1973	G.T. Chiene	1990	W.M. Johnstone
1974	J.H. Ness		

SANDY WATSON TROPHY

Inaugurated by the Society in 1989 in memory of Sandy Watson who bequeathed to the Society a legacy of over £50,000.
To be played for by members aged 70 and over.

1989	D.A. Hill
1990	W.M. Johnstone

GRAHAM-SMITH MEMORIAL TROPHY

Presented to the Society in 1938 by Miss Elizabeth Graham-Smith in memory of her late father to be competed for annually by members who are over the age of 50 on the date of the competition.

1939	L.G. Brown	1965	A.L. Mclure
1940	A. Nicoll	1966	T.G. Duncanson
1941	H.M. Sturrock	1967	B. Anderson
1942	J. Airey	1968	W.A. Whitelaw
1943	J. Airey	1969	A.M. Fraser
1944	A.L. Cameron	1970	J.L. Walker
1945	H.W. Mills	1971	P. Whyte
1946	J.G. Cunningham	1972	L.R. Tweedie
1947	C.E. Salveson	1973	R. Lamond
1948	A.R. Muirhead	1974	T.A. Fairbairn
1949	D.J. Colvin	1975	D.N. Maxwell
1950	N. Montgomery	1976	A.F. Anderson
1951	J.Y. Sutherland	1977	R.M. Knox
1952	J.A. Wright	1978	P. Whyte
1953	T.D. Adie	1979	T.A. Stanton
1954	D.C. Law	1980	J.R. Muir
1955	R.G. Manson	1981	A.A. Gunn
1956	A.R. Muirhead	1982	J.G. Mitchell
1957	C. Hastings	1983	L.J.S. Houston
1958	A.A. Lumley &	1984	J. Watson Forbes
	W.A. Davidson	1985	T.A. Buttery
1959	A.W. Scott	1986	R.G. Robertson
1960	K. Paterson Brown	1987	A. Stewart
1961	A.K. Allan	1988	G.B. Whyte
1962	N.A. Gray	1989	E.D. Hood
1963	A. Watson	1990	A.N. Gooding
1964	E.J. Petrie		

INCHES PUTTER

Presented to the Society in May 1898 by the then Captain, James H. Inches, to mark the occasion of the opening of the New Green (as it was then designated) at Barnton Gate in May 1898.

Awarded to the player returning the best scratch score in the summer meeting.

Year	Winner	Year	Winner
1899	G. MacGregor	1929	A.G. Thornton
1900	D. Currie	1930	G.T. Chiene
1901	D. Currie	1931	G.T. Chiene
1902	D. Currie	1932	R.M. Carnegie
1903	J.A.W. Anderson	1933	O.G. Miller
1904	A.D. Ferguson	1934	R. Kay
1905	R. Kay Jr	1935	K.F. Gibb
1906	E.F. Currie	1936	J.A. Shore
1907	D. Currie	1937	J.S. Graham
1908	R. Kay Jr	1938	A.F. Simpson
1909	A.D. Ferguson	1939	W.A. Whitelaw
1910	A.D. Ferguson	1940	
1911	D. Currie	1941	
1912	R. Todd	1942	
1913	T. Stevenson	1943	
1914	T. Stevenson	1944	
1915		1945	
1916		1946	J.H. Lamb
1917		1947	J.R. Ness
1918		1948	C.H. Johnston
1919	J.J. Brown	1949	G.T. Chiene
1920	W.A.S. Douglas	1950	A.M.M. Bucher
1921	A.L. Robson	1951	W.A. Whitelaw
1922	G. Romanes	1952	W.A. Whitelaw
1923	A. Burn-Murdoch	1953	C.N. Hastings
1924	A.L. Robson	1954	A. Macdonald Fraser
1925	J. Moir	1955	G.G. Fowler
1926	A.M. Macdonald	1956	R.G. Manson
1927	H.D. Fairbairn	1957	L.S. Hinchcliffe
1928	D. Rodger	1958	T.D. Hay

1959	D.F. Macrae	1976	P.J. Burnet
1960	T.A.F. Noble		M.R.S. Bateman
1961	T.G. Mitchell	1977	P.M.B. Bucher
1962	N.A. Gray	1978	P.M.B. Bucher
1963	L.S. Hinchcliffe	1979	A.N. Williamson
1964	R.J. Normand	1980	A.F. Brown
1965	C.N. Hastings	1981	A.G.G. Miller
1966	R.H.J. Mackie	1982	P.M.B. Bucher
1967	G.E. Robertson	1983	P.M.B. Bucher
1968	P.G.H. Younie	1984	A.F. Brown
1969	R.P. White	1985	A.G.G. Miller
1970	P.G.H. Younie	1986	E.M. Donaldson
1971	J.G. Mitchell	1987	A.G.G. Miller
1972	R.A. Davie	1988	J.C. Liddel
1973	P.M.B. Bucher	1989	A.D. Carnie
1974	P.M.B. Bucher	1990	A.G.G. Miller
1975	P.M.B. Bucher		

SUMMER MEETING
THE MAITLAND BOWL

Presented to the Society in 1899 by Miss Ramsay Gibson Maitland who was given the honorary position of patroness of the Society.
Awarded to the member returning the best net score in the summer meeting.

1899	R. Kay Jr.	1931	W. Shiel
1900	W.H. Nicholson	1932	J.P. Stewart
1901	F.M. Johnston	1933	O.G. Miller
1902	D.A. Callender	1934	R. Kay
1903	E.R. Boase	1935	J.B. Cormack
1904	J. Lawson	1936	W. Wallace
1905	G. Moncrieff	1937	J. Field
1906	A. Campbell	1938	H.C. Mccrostie
1907	D.A. Clapperton	1939	R.M. Hamilton
1908	R. Gibb	1940	
1909	J. Raeburn	1941	
1910	T. Ainslie	1942	
1911	J. Pourie	1943	
1912	A.M. Macrobert	1944	
1913	F.G. Bucher	1945	
1914	E.R. Boase	1946	H.L.C. Guthrie
1915		1947	W.F.G. Normand
1916		1948	J.Y. Erskine
1917		1949	A.J. Dobbie
1918		1950	J.A. Crawford
1919	W.M. Whitelaw	1951	M.M. Baird
1920	J.S. Graham	1952	J.R.G. Shaw
1921	O.R. Levey	1953	A.W. Wright
1922	R. Butchart	1954	A.MacD. Fraser
1923	R.L. Macdonald	1955	J. Hair
1924	J.B. Watson	1956	A. Smart
1925	K. Murray	1957	E.G. Stoddart
1926	R. Jamieson	1958	W.J. Shaw
1927	W.G. Cowan	1959	J.A.L. Chapman
1928	J. Allan	1960	T.A.F. Noble
1929	E.A. Burn Callander	1961	J.D. Cunningham
1930	D.C. Reid	1962	C.A. Crole

1963	L.S. Hinchcliffe	1977	L.R. Tweedie
1964	R.J. Normand	1978	H.H. Millar
1965	J.G. Morrison	1979	M.B. Auld
1966	I.W.H. Leslie	1980	H.N. Mcphail
1967	K.L. Younie	1981	T. Ballantine
1968	P.G.H. Younie	1982	David S. Reid
1969	R.G.C. Smith	1983	J.G. Cochrane
1970	I.D.K. Cameron	1984	A.D. Mackay
1971	A.A.B. Sharp	1985	J.A. Crerar
1972	J.K. Millar	1986	R. Summers
1973	P. Whyte	1987	A.F. Nixon
1974	P.C. Millar	1988	A. Skinner
1975	J.G. Aitchison	1989	R. Mathieson
1976	P.J. Burnet	1990	J.W. Elliott

STABLEFORD COMPETITION
RAF CUP

Presented to the Society in 1957 by the Rev. Dr A. McHardie who was Chaplain to King George VI.

It was first played for in 1964 as a Stableford Competition.

1958	A.A. Lumley	1970	H.H. Millar
	N.A. Gray	1971	O.P. Laidlaw
	J.A. Wright	1972	R.L. Macdonald
1959	W. Clark	1973	G.S.P. Bain
1960	N.M. Blair	1974	D.H.R. Ness
	C.H. Davidson	1975	R.G.C. Smith
	T.I.L. Burns	1976	H.H. Millar
	D.N. Maxwell	1977	A.M. Smith
1961	N.A. Gray	1978	W.B. Ritchie
	A. Smart	1979	W. Brown
	D.N. Maxwell	1980	I.W.H. Leslie
	J. Ross	1981	E.T. Kerr
	A.W.D. Moodie	1982	K.J.F. Scotland
1962	D.S. Robb	1983	A.R. Gilchrist
1963	D.I.K. Mcleod	1984	A. Stewart
1964	J.R.D. Murray	1985	E.D.E. Dobbs
1965	J.A.L. Chapman	1986	W.M. Johnstone
1966	W.B. Abbott	1987	G.C. Grieve
1967	H.J.L. Allan	1988	A.J. Cole
1968	J.H. Ness	1989	J.G. Banks
1969	A.C. Stepney	1990	A.S. Kemp

FOURSOMES BOGEY COMPETITION
HENRY R. STURROCK TROPHY

Bogey Foursomes Competition. Presented to the Society in 1959 by Henry R. Sturrock who had been Captain from 1945–47.

1954	A.S. Nichol & I.D.K. Cameron	1968	I.M. Ferguson & G.E. Robertson
1955	A.R. Mcinroy & M.H. Cullen	1969	W.A Mccallum & A.C. Stepney
	R.G. Manson & R.A. Inglis	1970	A.R. Smith & M.J. Sands
1956	J.I.M. Meikle & P.F.S Kittermaster	1971	M.G. Pearson & J.R.B. Livingstone
1957	R. Young & P.S. Ballantine	1972	W. Clark & J.D. Cochrane
	J.A. Wright & G.G.P. Dodds	1973	W.G.F. Carnie & A.P. Gray
1958	J.I.M. Meikle & P.F.S. Kittermaster	1974	H. Henderson & W.J. Oates
1959	G.G.I. Cameron & J.A.L. Chapman	1975	W.R.G. Kerr & D.S. Reid
1960	W.F.G. Norman & J.W.St.C. Scott	1976	M.M. Baird & L.Y. Anderson
1961	F.G. Dewar & W.O. Trotter	1977	I.W. Hall & T.I.K. Burns
1962	V.W. Thomson & J.D. Cochrane	1978	N.A. Gray & R.R. Orchard
1963	W.G.F. Carnie & G. Kay	1979	A.A. Hughes & H. Henderson
1964	F.G. Dewar & A.J.D. Allison	1980	G.A. Tennant & F.V. Ellvers
1965	I.W. Hall & N. Mclean	1981	C.R. Johnston & W.S.G. Russell
1966	R. Young & P.S. Ballantine	1982	L.C. Young & J.A. Kirkpatrick
1967	R.R. Orchard & A.O. Kay	1983	R. Mcvitie & P. Whyte

1984	J.W.St.C. Scott & R.R. Orchard	1989	I.A.C. Whyte & W.W Stewart
1985	D.N. Maxwell & J.H. Mutch	1990	G.A. Tennant & F.V. Ellvers
1986	R.W. Holroyd & W.D. Fraser	1926	J.F. Carnegie W. Wallace
1987	E.D. Hood & A.A. Hughes		
1988	E.D. Hood & A.A. Hughes		

VICTORIA CUP

Presented to the Society in 1901 by Edward Bruce the Captain at that time.
Awarded to the winner of the Bogey Competition.

1901	J.H. Hood	1934	R.A. Morrison
1902	W. Elder	1935	A.W. Bannerman
1903	J.M. Rutherford	1936	S.J. Hall
1904	H.C. Tillard	1937	J. Field
1905	H.D. Thomas	1938	S.J. Hall
1906	G.C. Stewart	1939	W.A. Baxter
1907	D. Currie	1940	
1908	A.B. Thomson	1941	
1909	R. Gibb	1942	
1910	A.D. Ferguson	1943	
1911	A.B. Dawson	1944	
1912	G. Hart	1944	
1913	T. Stevenson	1945	
1914	J.M. Usher	1946	J.S. Clarkson
1915		1947	A. Dunbar
1916		1948	A.F. Simpson
1917		1949	C. Hastings
1918		1950	A. Hawley
1919	R. Kay Jr.	1951	W.M. Mackay
1920	J.P.S. Miller	1952	T.C. Scott
1921	A.L. Robson	1953	A.W. Wright
1922	E.R. Boase	1954	J.A. Lang
1923	E.A. Burn-Callander	1955	N.W. Thomson
1924	J.S. Graham	1956	A. Watt
1925	J.A. Wright	1957	G.G.P. Dodds
1926	F.J.B. Makie	1958	T.I.L. Burns
1927	G. Graham Davidson	1959	A.R. Smith
1928	E.S. Banks	1960	A.W. Wright
1929	R.N. Finlay	1961	T.G. Duncanson
1930	J.F. Strachan	1962	D.N. Maxwell
1931	G.G. Smith	1963	D.N. Maxwell
1932	J.S. Graham	1964	M.T. Green
1933	A.D. Lambert	1965	R. Young

1966	A.E.R. Petrie	1979	A.D. Carnie
1967	R.W. Holroyd	1980	J. Elder
1968	G.E. Robertson	1981	W.S.G. Russell
1969	I.D. Blackhall	1982	J.A. Kirkpatrick
1970	F.G. Dewar	1983	G.A. Tennant
1971	A. Douglas	1984	O.P. Laidlaw
1972	H.J. Denholm	1985	W.J. Scholes
1973	R.B. Law	1986	I.E. Cochran
1974	I.W. Hall	1987	N. Fort
1975	J.B. Burke	1988	T.C. Bell
1976	J.G. Mitchell	1989	D.S. Bell
1977	W.K. Moncur	1990	A.G.G. Miller
1978	A.D. Carnie		

AUTUMN MEETING
CAIRNS MEDAL

Presented to the Society in 1839 by G. Cairns for annual competition on the Musselburgh Links where the Society was then located.

Awarded to the member returning the lowest scratch score in the autumn meeting.

1839	S. Aitken	1870	D. Croall
1840	S. Aitken	1871	R. Chambers
1841	S. Aitken	1872	A. Usher
1842	G. Brown	1873	A. Whyte
1843	A. Scott	1874	A. Whyte
1844	G. Brown	1875	A. Whyte
1845	W.H. Cameron	1876	A.M.H. Bryson
1846	S. Aitken	1877	R. Wallace
1847	A. Aitken	1878	J.R. Whitecross
1848	R.T. Galloway	1879	A.M.H. Bryson
1849	J. Miller	1880	W.G.B. Loxsom
1850		1881	A. Douglas
1851		1882	A. Douglas
1852		1883	A. Usher
1853	J. Greenhill	1884	J. Law
1854	R. Clark	1885	W.G.B. Bloxsom
1855	R. Chambers	1886	D. Maclaren
1856	R. Clark	1887	D. Maclaren
1857	R. Clark	1888	A.A. Thomson
1858	R. Chambers	1889	D. Maclaren
1859	R. Chambers	1890	J. Taylor
1860	J. Greenhill	1891	J. Taylor
1861	J.W. Young	1892	J. Taylor
1862	W. Lees	1893	T.T. Gray
1863	W. Lees	1894	W.B. Taylor
1864	D. Croall	1895	T.T. Gray
1865	A. Young	1896	T.T. Gray
1866	C. Mccraig	1897	W.B. Taylor
1867	W. Caldwell	1898	W.B. Taylor
1868	W. Lees	1899	A.D.M. Mackenzie
1869	J.T. Cunningham	1900	W.B. Taylor

1901	D. Currie	1941	
1902	D. Currie	1942	
1903	W.B. Taylor	1943	
1904	D. Currie	1944	
1905	J.C.M. Bell	1945	
1906	R. Kay Jr.	1946	J.R. Mcintosh
1907	WM. Macrae	1947	R.W. Jenkins
1908	WM. Macrae	1948	J.W.St.C. Scott
1909	C. Hay	1949	C.R.D. Lees
1910	A.R. Simpson	1950	A.M.M. Bucher
1911	T. Stevenson	1951	J.M. Cowan
1912	R. Kay Jr.	1952	R.M. Lees
1913	A.M. Mackay	1953	W.A. Whitelaw
1914		1954	J.A. Lang
1915		1955	G.G. Fowler
1916		1956	R.M. Lees
1917		1957	A.G. Donald
1918		1958	A.R. Mcinroy
1919	R. Cairns Jr.	1959	L.S. Hinchcliffe
1920	J. Moir	1960	A.G. Donald
1921	A.D.F. Torrance	1961	R.M. Lees
1922	A. Burn-murdoch	1962	T.C. Scott
1923	A.M. Macdonald	1963	J. Chienne Jr.
1924	A.L. Robson	1964	P.R. Bryce
1925	E.B. Dickson	1965	L.S. Hinchcliffe
1926	R. Cairns Jr.	1966	R.A. Davie
1927	A. Burn-Murdoch	1967	R.R. Jack
1928	H.D. Fairbairn	1968	G.E. Robertson
1929	J. Chiene	1969	J.W.H. Fairweather
1930	R.M. Carnegie	1970	F.G. Dewar
1931	R.M. Carnegie	1971	I.W. Hall
1932	J.S. Graham	1972	R.P. White
1933	G. Romanes	1973	R.P. White
1934	R.M. Carnegie	1974	R. Reid Jack
1935	G.W. Mackie	1975	R.H.J. Mackie
1936	N.E.D. Haggard	1976	G.E. Robertson
1937	J.S. Graham	1977	A.D. Carnie
1938	W.A. Cochrane	1978	A.D. Carnie
1939		1979	A.F. Brown
1940		1980	G. Mcclung

1981	A.D. Carnie	1985	A.G.G. Miller
1982	A.F. Brown	1986	K.W. Aitken
	C.N. Hastings	1987	D.C.Grieve
	K.W. Aitken	1988	J.S. Hodge
	R.W. Rowberry	1989	J.H. Bryce
1983	A.G.G. Miller	1990	A.G.G. Miller
1984	A.F. Brown		

HAY MEDAL

Presented to the Society in 1882 by the then Captain H.S.A.L. Hay.
Awarded to the member returning the lowest net score in the autumn
meeting.

1882	M.M.M. Prain	1914	
1883	W. Braid	1915	
1884	A.M. Brown	1916	
1885	W.G. Bloxom	1917	
1886	D. Maclaren	1918	
1887	C.M. Maxwell	1919	A.G. Thornton
1888	C.N. Cowper	1920	G.W. Shearer
1889	R.L. Macdonald	1921	W. Annan
1890	J.D. Paterson	1922	G.W. Harper
1891	W. Paxton	1923	W.A. Fleming
1892	J. Shaw	1924	W.A. Fleming
1893	J.A. Adair	1925	J. Martin
1894	D. Foulis	1926	J.F. Carnegie W. Wallace
1895	J.A. Adair	1927	W. Hutton
1896	W.W. Macfarlane	1928	P. Galloway
1897	D.N. Cotton	1929	K.F. Gibb
1898	G. Cotton	1930	G.R. Lawson
1899	J.C. Johnstone	1931	J.S. Fraser
1900	A. Guthrie	1932	J.S. Graham
1901	C. Tweedie	1933	G. Romanes
1902	W. Adams Jr.	1934	A.S. Bruce
1903	D.S. Duncan	1935	J.A. Wright
1904	A. Kyle	1936	N. Montgomery
1905	A.G. Renwick	1937	J.S. Graham
1906	A.M. Mackay	1938	W.A. Cochrane
1907	L.S. Shennan	1939	
1908	R. Butchart	1940	
1909	W. Geoghegan	1941	
1910	D. Somerville	1942	
1911	A.M. Mackay	1943	
1912	C.H. Robson	1944	
1913	D.L. Brown	1945	

1946	J.B.W. Christie	1969	J.W.H. Fairweather
1947	A.D. Crichton	1970	A.M.G. Russell
1948	C.R.D. Leeds	1971	A.F. Simpson
1949	J.Y. Sutherland	1972	C.W. Black
1950	A.D. Mackenzie	1973	J.D. Cochrane
1951	J.M. Cowan	1974	J.K. Millar
1952	G.G.P. Dodds	1975	D.M. Baxendine
1953	R.J. Normand	1976	G.A. Scott
1954	I.W. Hall	1977	T.I.L. Burns
1955	T.I.L. Burns	1978	R.W. Stirling
1956	G.C. Summers	1979	A.L.M. Cuthbert
1957	I.A. Ross	1980	G. Mcclung
1958	R.R. Orchard	1981	W. Clark
1959	A.R. Smith	1982	N.C. Thomson
1960	A. Blair	1983	A.F. Gunn
1961	A.W.D. Moodie	1984	J. Nicolson
1962	E.R. Mcleod	1985	A.N. Gooding
1963	D.N. Maxwell	1986	J.K. Millar
1964	G. Young	1987	D.C. Grieve
1965	I.M. Ferguson	1988	J.S. Hodge
1966	J.A.R. Macphail	1989	J.H. Bryce
1967	R.R. Jack	1990	T.A. Buttery
1968	K.M.C. Gray		

LINDSAY ANDERSON MEMORIAL TROPHY

Presented to the Society in 1987 by The Royal Bank of Scotland in memory of Lindsay Anderson who gave valuable service both to the Society as a member in match and handicap administration and as the Treasurer and Secretary of The Royal Bank of Scotland Golf Club.

1987	T.A. Buttery	1989	T.C. Bell
1988	A. Skinner	1990	G.C. Grieve

GRAND FLEET CUP

Presented to the Society in 1920 by the Officers of the Grand Fleet in recognition of the privilege which the Officers had enjoyed during 1914 to 1919 of playing over the course. The same Officers presented a Grand Fleet Cup to The Royal Burgess Golfing Society.

It is played for, in late October, by the winners of the Tom Stevenson Cup, Gold Medal, Ladies Cup, Inches Putter, Maitland Bowl, RAF Cup, Cairns Medal, Hay Medal, Victoria Cup and Lindsay Anderson Memorial Trophy.

1920	C.C. Robson	1948	J.A. Jack
1921	J.S. Barker	1949	C.R.D. Leeds
1922	G. Romanes	1950	W.C. Hopekirk
1923	A.L. Robson	1951	A.F. Simpson
1924	I.R. Macleod	1952	R.M. Lees
1925	J. Martin	1953	A.W. Wright
1926	R. Jamieson	1954	J.A. Lang
1927	H.L.C. Guthrie	1955	T.I.L. Burns
1928	H.L.C. Guthrie	1956	R.M. Lees
1929	J.F. Reekie	1957	R.M. Lees
1930	G.T. Chiene	1958	A.R. Mcinroy
1931	G.A. Fraser	1959	A.R. Smith
1932	J.S. Graham	1960	A.G. Donald
1933	G. Romanes	1961	F.G. Dewar
1924	J.A. Shore	1962	N.A. Gray
1935	J.B. Cormack	1963	D.N. Maxwell
1936	S.J. Hall	1964	R.J. Normand
1937	D.W. Gordon	1965	C.N. Hastings
1938	W.A. Cochrane	1966	R.A. Davie
1939		1967	W.B.M. Laird
1940		1968	G.E. Robertson
1941		1969	P.M.B. Bucher
1942		1970	A.P. Gray
1943		1971	A.A.B. Sharp
1944		1972	J.K. Millar
1945		1973	P. Whyte
1946	T.G. Duncanson	1974	I.W. Hall
1947	A. Dunbar	1975	J.B. Burke

1976	P.G.H. Younie	1984	A.F. Brown
1977	A.H. James	1985	W.J. Scholes
1978	W.B. Ritchie	1986	J.K. Miller
1979	A.D. Carnie	1987	G.C. Grieve
1980	G. Mcclung	1988	A. Skinner
1981	A.D. Carnie	1989	P.G. Renton
1982	J.A. Kirkpatrick	1990	T.A. Buttery
1983	A.F. Gunn		

GILMOUR CUP

Presented to the Society by Hugh Gilmour who had been Captain from 1895–96.
Awarded to the winners of the Winter Foursomes Hole and Hole.

1902	M.M. Craig & A.H. Callender	1920	J. Moir & A.M. Macdonald
1903	F.M. Johnston & A. Morrison	1921	A. Burn–Murdoch & J.S. Parker
1904	R. Todd & A.M. Bucher	1922	A.R. Muirhead & N.T. Scott
1905	J.A. Robertson & G.W. Robertson	1923	R.A. Bruce & A.D.F. Torrance
1906	J.A. Robertson & L.S. Shennan	1924	A.L. Robson & J. Cairns
1907	I.R. Macleod & J.C. Lane	1925	A.M. Macdonald & G.W. Shearer
1908	A.M. Bucher & J.G. Graham	1926	C. Hay & G.L. Hay
1909	C. Hay & R.A. Bruce	1927	R.N. Finlay & L. Hill Watson
1910	R.W. Pentland & E. Bruce Jr	1928	J. Cairns & W.A. Ireland
1911	R. Todd & D.R. Brown	1929	R.M. Carnegie & J. Chiene
1912	D. Drummond & T.D. Wilson	1930	J.R. Watson & D. Rodger
1913	R. Todd & D.R. Brown	1931	J.A. Bruce & G.T. Chiene
1914	D. Calder & F.B. Allan	1932	A.G. Thornton & H.R. Sturrock
1915		1933	C.J. Nicolson & D.F. Wishart
1916			
1917		1934	J.S. Graham & A.D. Lambert
1918			
1919			

1935	J.A. Shore & H.D. Fairbairn	1958	C.M. Meek & W.M. Tait
1936	A.D. Lambert & J.S. Graham	1959	A.G. Donald & T.M.P. Taylor
1937	C.E. Salveson & J.S. Graham	1960	L.Y. Anderson & A.K. Allan
1938	J.C. Smith & W.A. Cochrane	1961	R.D. Cairns & P.L. Stewart
1939	J.C. Smith & W.A. Cochrane	1962	J. Letham & J.D. Cochrane
1940		1963	D.N. Doull & D.N. Maxwell
1941			
1942		1964	A.G. Donald & T.M.P. Taylor
1943			
1944		1965	W.R.G. Kerr & D.S. Reid
1945			
1946		1966	A.R. Anderson & P.G.H. Younie
1947	R.W. Jenkins & G.G. Fowler	1967	A.R. Anderson & P.G.H. Younie
1948	A. Macdonald Fraser & T.W.W. Davie	1968	W.O. Trotter & F.G. Dewar
1949	C. Hastings & G. Kay	1969	S.L. Anderson & G.C. Summers
1950	C.R.D. Leeds & A.A. Lumley	1970	A.R. Smith & M.J. Sands
1951	R.M. Lees & M.H. Cullen	1971	R.M. Lees & D.G.R. Robertson
1952	A.A. Lumley & C.R.D. Leeds	1972	T.G. Lamb & J.G. Banks
1953	C.M. Meek & W.M. Tait	1973	R.M. Lees & R.M. Rowberry
1954	J.W. Sands & D.C. Law	1974	I.W. Hall & T.I.L. Burns
1955	C.M. Meek & W.M. Tait	1975	I.W. Hall & T.I.L. Burns
1956	C.M. Meek & W.M. Tait	1976	A.G. Donald & W.A. Simpson
1957	R.G. Manson & R.A. Inglis	1977	I.A.C. Whyte & J.D. Crerar

1978	A.P. Gray & R.I. Macdonald	1985	G.W. Simpson & D.L. Millar
1979	A. Petrie & J.D. Crerar	1986	D.W. Holton & A.R. Steedman
1980	I.A.C. Whyte & W.W. Stewart	1987	D.C. Grieve & G.C. Grieve
1981	R.A. Davie & A.G.G. Miller	1988	D.W. Ferguson & M. Gilhooley
1982	R.M. Sinclair & D.M. Simpson	1989	D.M. Kidd & D.A. Hill
1983	R.A. Davie & A.G.G. Miller	1990	J.I. Wilson & M.L. Cowan
1984	R.M. Lees & R.M. Rowberry		

SERVICES CUP

Presented to the Society by the Services Members in 1911.
Awarded to the member with the best net 36 holes aggregate in the Spring,
Summer and Autumn Meetings.

1911	F.g. Bucher	1940	I.T. Whitehead
1912	R. Todd	1941	
1913	T. Stevenson	1942	
1914	T. Stevenson	1943	
1915		1944	
1916		1945	
1917		1946	W.F.G. Normand
1918		1947	A.W. Bannerman
1919	D.A. Clapperton:	1948	J.W. St. C. Scott
	H.B. Murdock :	1949	J.Y. Sutherland
	A.G. Thornton	1950	J.A. Crawford
1920	J.S. Graham :	1951	W. Carnie
	W.A.S. Douglas	1952	R.M. Lees
1921	A.L. Robson	1953	R.J. Normand
1922	A.F. Sandeman	1954	J.H. Ness
1923	E.A. Burn-Callander	1955	T.I.L. Burns
1924	J. Aikman	1956	T.G. Duncanson
1925	J.C. Smith Jr	1957	E.G. Stoddart
1926	R. Jamieson	1958	R. Young
1927	R.S. Campbell	1959	R.M. Lees
1928	J. Russell Watson	1960	D.S. Mackenzie
1929	E.A. Burn-Callender	1961	J.D. Cunningham
1930	C.C. Mitchell	1962	A.M.M. Bucher
1931	D. Graham Munro	1963	F.F. Kellow
1932	J.S. Graham	1964	M.J. Sands
1933	O.G. Miller	1965	I.M. Ferguson
1934	W.F.M. Whitelaw	1966	J.A.R. Macphail
1935	K.F. Gibb	1967	K.L. Younie
1936	W. Wallace	1968	J.F. Mendl
1937	D.W. Gordon	1969	R.M.S. Allison
1938	J. Halliday Croome	1970	P.G.H. Younie
1939		1971	A.I.F. Cochrane

1972	R.R. Jack	1982	David S. Reid
1973	N.A. Gray	1983	I.C. Scotland
1974	P.C. Millar	1984	J. Nicolson :
1975	G.A. Latta		I.T. Whitehead
1976	A.L.M. Cuthbert	1985	A.N. Gooding
1977	T.I.L. Burns	1986	E.G. Sangster
1978	R.W. Stirling	1987	D.C. Grieve
1979	J.G.S. Kirkland	1988	J.C. Liddel
1980	N. Lessels :	1989	R. Mathieson
	R.J. Normand	1990	A.S. Kemp
1981	W. Clark		

ROBERT KAY CUP

Acquired by the Society in 1973 from a legacy bequeathed by Robert Kay. Awarded to the member with the best aggregate of two net scores in monthly Medals.

1973	I.S. Morrison	1982	I.S. Morton
1974	R.D. Cairns	1983	A.R. Gilchrist
1975	O.L. Balfour	1984	I.T. Whitehead
1976	R.S. Davie	1985	V.F. Barnett
1977	G.E. Robertson		A.G.G. Miller
1978	D. Sharp	1986	G.C. Grieve
1979	J.G. Clark	1987	W.W. Stewart
	A.M. Duff	1988	A.G. Young
1980	N.C. Thomson	1989	A.J. Morrice
1981	J.G. Banks	1990	W.F. Malcolm
	D.B. Donaldson		

APPENDIX 2

The Burgess Connection

At a centenary dinner of the Society in 1861 the Captain asserted that its origin was political, within a few years of the '45, and that within the old Burgess Club were members with embittered Jacobite memories of that disaster. They adhered to the Lost Cause, could not bring themselves to drink to the health of its supporters, and in a body eventually withdrew, to found the Bruntsfield Links Golf Club. Without supporting confirmation from a trustworthy source this assertion could be set aside, and indeed it would be incautious to give it undue prominence, but we must declare that nothing is more likely in Edinburgh at that time, vibrant still with Jacobite/Hanoverian dissension.

To disagree with the sadistic tendencies of the Green Committee, the incompetence of the Secretary and the lunacy of the Handicapping Committee was one thing, but to disagree with the heresies of Whig or Tory was another. Furthermore, the particular name 'Burgess' does not appear in the minutes of that Society until 1787, before which date they refer to the 'Edinburgh Golfing Society', or the 'Society of Golfers in and about Edinburgh', which could include the Bruntsfield breakaways.

The argument in favour of original and mutual identity goes far to explain a remarkable series of apparent coincidences, or at least parallel actions, which have forcibly impressed me from time to time while in full pursuit of this Bruntsfield history. In pondering them I have been impelled to think there must be early loyalties as well as neighbourly connections to account for them, for the occasions have been more than mere convenience would require. For example, the two Societies were active to preserve Bruntsfield Links (in which joint efforts, it must be confessed, other golfing societies doubtless played their part): in 1790, within a week or two, each declared for a uniform and was badged: at the Links in 1818 they commemorated a new 'Union' hole with a match, and thereafter dined together with notable formality and friendship: in the Bruntsfield minutes are decisions to minimise or avoid fixtures with other clubs, even the historic 'Musselburgh' being excluded, but Burgess was not: at Musselburgh, when Bruntsfield's new clubhouse was being built and the members were temporarily homeless, Burgess with great generosity opened the doors of its new clubhouse and made them honorary members forby: in 1892, at a time of growing dissatisfaction with the Musselburgh green, there was even a proposal of amalgamation, the disposal of one clubhouse and the sharing of the other. For the Boys' Championship of 1937 Bruntsfield granted the contestants every facility, in the clubhouse and on the green, and Burgess reciprocated in aid of the consequently dispossessed of Bruntsfield.

Perhaps most appealing of all those instances is the last move of all, from Musselburgh back to Edinburgh, when intriguing coincidences might here be observed, two historic golfing societies quit Musselburgh, where they are neighbours, at the same time, and separately settle in the same Edinburgh estate, at the same time, and in it make two new golf courses, contiguously, at the same time: and a couple of years later each elects the Captain of the other to Honorary Membership.

As for vexatious foundation dates, about which there is never a lack of critics and only the balance of probability to sustain them, for the dates are inferential, it so happens that the earliest published minute of the Bruntsfield Society is of 10 June 1787, the very year when the name 'Burgess' first appears in the Burgess minutes. From this coincidence too much can be inferred. The Burgess *Chronicle* cogently argues the case for its 1735, and a Bruntsfield minute of 1790 categorically states the case for 1760, or earlier. It seems to me, and I advance this opinion with extreme diffidence, that they were both one originally, and have continued to be so, each in its own way.

Index